EMPLOYER CONCENTRATION IN
LOCAL LABOR MARKETS

Employer Concentration in Local Labor Markets

By

ROBERT L. BUNTING

Chapel Hill

THE UNIVERSITY OF NORTH CAROLINA PRESS

TO BEACHY

ACKNOWLEDGMENTS

This study is the result of work that took place over several years. The help I received over these years from one person, H. Gregg Lewis, was so great as to make it impossible to overstate my obligation to him. It would be tedious in the extreme to point out the many places in this volume that reflect his touch—it would be a simpler task to list the pages he did not influence. I do not wish to suggest that he bears any part of the responsibility for such shortcomings as this study may have; I *do* want to state unequivocally that it is an infinitely better job than it would have been without his aid. I am deeply grateful for the time he spent on my problems and for the many contributions he made to their solution.

Also, a large debt of gratitude is owed to the staff of the Bureau of Old-Age and Survivors Insurance of the Department of Health, Education, and Welfare. Their data serve as the core of this study and their cooperation, over and over again, was indispensable to the kind of understanding needed to make effective use of these data. Within the Bureau, B. J. Mandel, former Chief of the Statistics Branch, Robert Heller, Saul Hearn, and Ira Rifkind were especially generous in their assistance.

The major portion of this study was done while I was a member of the faculty of the University of North Carolina at Chapel Hill. I discussed my work with so many friends at that institution that—with the exception of Dudley Cowden, whom I exploited more than most—I shall not try to name names. To all of these former colleagues go my thanks. Also, Juanita M. Kreps went beyond the call of duty in carefully working through an early draft of the complete manuscript;

Edgar P. Hickman read the section of the appendix entitled "A Test of Monopsony Theory" and made several suggestions concerning statistical interpretation. Frank Verlinden was helpful in putting the data into useful form, while Goldston Harris, Jim Gooding, and Bill Godwin were most conscientious in their efforts with early hand computations. More recently, Carol Vacek, Sandra Lehrman, and Dorothy Hinman hammered out a final typewritten draft despite full-time responsibilities elsewhere.

It is no idle coincidence that the final paragraph in the acknowledgments of so many academic efforts starts out the same way: "Finally, to my long-suffering wife, for encouragement, patience, proof-reading, typing services, etc." Wives invariably contribute much and bear more than their share of the variety of pain costs associated with such undertakings. My case is no exception—if anything, my debt is greater and my gratitude more fully-earned. And so, for encouragement, patience, proof-reading, typing services, etc., go my special thanks. . . .

TABLE OF CONTENTS

LIST OF TABLES

LIST OF FIGURES

EMPLOYER CONCENTRATION IN
LOCAL LABOR MARKETS

CHAPTER I

CONCENTRATION AND MONOPSONY IN
LABOR MARKETS

1. THE RELEVANCE OF CONCENTRATION TO MONOPSONY

One need not be very familiar with the writings of professional economists to be aware of great differences among them on matters of national labor policy. It is clear that some substantial part of these differences arises from different beliefs about the degree of competition among employers in labor markets. To the extent that this is so, the point at issue is subject to scientific analysis. And to the extent that empirical investigation can resolve the differences, greater consensus among economists can safely be predicted on a wide range of important policy problems: minimum wages, collective bargaining, fair labor standards, and the like.

The conflict in views held by economists with regard to the extent of labor monopsony[1] in the United States seems to be, primarily, a reflection of differences in belief about the structural characteristics of labor markets. On the one hand, there is the view that many markets in the United States are "dominated" by one or a few relatively large

---

1. Monopsony is used in this paper as a generic term that covers not only simple monopsony theory as it is commonly given in the economics literature (see Shorey Peterson, *Economics* [1st. ed. rev.; New York: Henry Holt and Company, 1954], pp. 641-44) but also the more complicated monopsony-like theories (employers' associations or cartels, wage domination or leadership, labor oligopsony, kinky labor supply curves, etc.) that "assume" that some "profit-maximizing" unit acts as though the supply of labor to itself were less than infinitely elastic. See as illustrations: Adam Smith, *The Wealth of Nations* ("Everyman's Library"; London: J. M. Dent and Sons, Ltd., 1937), I, 57-78; Paul H. Douglas, "Wage Theory and Wage Policy," *International Labour Review*, XXXIX, No. 3 (1939), 319-59; M. Bronfenbrenner, "Applications of the Discontinuous Oligopoly Demand Curve," *Journal of Political Economy*, XLIX (June, 1940), 420-27; K. W. Rothschild, *The Theory of Wages* (Oxford: Basil Blackwell, 1956), pp. 94-105.

firms; the expression "the company town" appears frequently in the writings of those who are sympathetic with this view. The contrary notion is that such labor market situations are not widespread, so that most workers in this country sell their services in markets characterized by competitive behavior among firms. The disagreement is obviously similar in many respects to that concerning the amount of product market monopoly in this country.

Until 1946 there were no readily available data which covered a large part of employment in the United States and which provided the distribution of firms by employment size in local labor markets. In that year, however, the Bureau of Old-Age and Survivors Insurance (BOASI) and the Office of Domestic Commerce jointly initiated a new series of bulletins; these bulletins contained county distributions of firms by employment-size categories, as well as industry and wage information. This publication program was continued unaltered through 1948 by which time the data had been improved and extended enough for them to serve as the basis for reasonably accurate estimates of labor market concentration. The purpose of this study is that of providing a set of such estimates for 1948; the hope is that they will contribute to the settlement of the disagreement among economists regarding labor market concentration, and hence labor monopsony, in the United States.

In the preceding paragraphs the words monopsony and concentration have been used rather loosely. It is important to see that they are not identical concepts—that they should not be used interchangeably. Concentration refers to a physical, observable, and describable characteristic of the market: high concentration exists when "a few" employers hire "a large percentage" of the workers in the market; low concentration exists when no single employer, or small group of employers together, hires a "significantly large" percentage of the labor force. The word "monopsony," on the other hand, refers to a condition that exists within the market; it describes the results of a type of market behavior among buyers leading to a wage complex the general level of which is below that which would have prevailed if those employers had been acting competitively. The hypothesis of central importance to this study relates market behavior to market structure: more precisely, it states that monopsony in labor markets is associated with high concentration of employees among employers.

It may be worth while to examine briefly the rationale underlying this hypothesis. Consider what shall be called a "local labor market" in which a certain group of employers are currently acting as buyers of a particular type of labor. The elasticity of supply of labor to this "local labor market" will be high if one condition is met: it is that there be an appreciable number of job opportunities offered by employers outside this "market" which are excellent substitutes in the eyes of the workers concerned. If this condition obtains there will be little incentive for the employers in the "local labor market" to engage in monopsonistic activity, for the high supply elasticity makes it certain that the monopsony gains will be small.

The validity of this analysis is quite independent of the extent to which most of the employment opportunities in this "market" are concentrated in one or a few employers. The point is that monopsonistic behavior can be successful only if what has been referred to as the "local labor market" is the *whole* market, in the sense that it includes all employment opportunities that the workers think of as good alternatives.

Suppose that this condition is satisfied; the local labor market has been defined in such a way that the elasticity of supply of labor to it is "low." The inelasticity of labor supply thus holds out the promise of monopsony gains to the employers. There will be an incentive to the employers to capture these gains, however, only if the costs of capturing them are not excessive. Capturing them necessarily means that the labor-purchasing firms exercise control over the market pressures urging them toward the competitive market position and move instead toward the pure monopsony market position; the more closely this latter position can be approximated, the greater the monopsony returns. Thus the pursuit of monopsony gain requires collective action—action involving tacit or explicit collusion—on the part of the employers. But such organizational activity is difficult—i.e., costly—and the difficulties increase the larger the number of employers concerned.[2] Thus concentration enters the theory as a de-

2. The labor market models, such as wage leadership, in which tacit collusion appears are almost universally discussed in terms that clearly indicate the assumed presence of concentration. Thus it might seem that the emphasis in the text upon the costliness of this type of behavior is unnecessary and, perhaps, mis-

terminant of the costs of collective action. And the concentration hypothesis—that, *ceteris paribus,* monopsonistic behavior is most likely to be observed where a few employers hire a large percentage of the relevant labor force—becomes the statement that monopsony is most likely to exist, given conditions of labor supply, where the potential net gains are greatest.

A comparative comment is again relevant; the above outline of the theoretical basis for this study closely parallels the theory of product market monopoly. The problems associated with defining the components of labor supply and the geographic extent of the labor market in the monopsony analysis have their counterparts in defining the product components of industry supply and the geographic extent of the product market. Concentration plays an identical role in the monopoly analysis; it is a major determinant of the cost of collective action on the part of sellers. This parallelism may helpfully be continued by pointing out that an important aim of the present study is that of beginning the process of building a body of concentration ratios for labor markets comparable with the established body of concentration data now available to students of product monopoly.[3]

It must immediately be recognized, however, that there is dissatisfaction with the concentration-monopoly hypothesis;[4]

---

leading. I believe, however, that this is the correct analytical approach. In any given market situation holding out the possibility of monopsonistic gain, the efficient means of obtaining those gains is through joint action of a straightforward type; the interested employers gather around a table and hammer out a common course of action. This process must involve the achievement of agreement on technical matters—such as the appropriate wage scales for various levels of activity in possibly quite diverse employment situations—as well as perhaps more difficult policy problems having to do with the best means of maximizing monopsony gains. (Should the emphasis be upon short- or long-term gains? How far below the competitive level may wages be pressed before other firms will be enticed into the market?) The point is that effective collective action requires communication and consensus, both of which have real economic costs attached. Bringing tacit collusion into this framework is based on the assumption that these costs do not disappear when less obvious methods of striving for common policies are adopted. Rather, one would expect that they rise, that the costs of obtaining a particular level of monopsony returns in any given set of market circumstances would be greater for those who try to operate under the handicap of indirect means of communication.

3. It is this aim which dictates the availability of an 84-page table containing much of the basic data analyzed in Chapter III. This table may be procured at no cost by writing to either the author, Robert L. Bunting, Department of Economics and Business Administration, Cornell College, Mount Vernon, Iowa, or to the publishers, The University of North Carolina Press, Chapel Hill, N.C.

4. Miller has expressed one version of this dissatisfaction in the following

furthermore, the empirical efforts to test it have enjoyed neither a large nor unambiguous measure of success.[5] It may be that the theory is deficient—that, for example, other necessary conditions remain unidentified—or, it may be that the empirical tests have been too crude. Whatever the nature of the unsolved problems in the area of product market monopoly, the meaning of this state of affairs for the relatively unexplored empirical area of monopsony is clear: the significance of findings on labor market concentration for the extent to which less-than-competitive wages obtain in labor markets is not known. Labor market concentration measures such as those of this study *may* be excellent indicators of monopsonistic behavior. On the other hand, the measures may be seriously inadequate because they do not encompass some important aspect of structure or because they fail altogether to identify other relevant variables of a non-structural character.

The point of the above discussion may be summarized briefly: this is a study of concentration in labor markets; the literature clearly indicates the belief of many economists that the degree of concentration is relevant to an analysis of monopsony and that measures such as those presented here point in the right direction; *but,* the relationship between these measures and the type of market behavior referred to as monopsony is imprecisely understood and awaits empirical

fashion: ''It is perhaps a sign of the immaturity of the science of economics that the notion should persist that the competitiveness of the economy or of a sector of the economy can ultimately be characterized by some single number or set of numbers.'' (John Perry Miller, ''Measures of Monopoly Power and Concentration: Their Economic Significance'' in National Bureau of Economic Research, *Business Concentration and Price Policy*, A Conference of the Universities-National Bureau Committee for Economic Research [Princeton: Princeton University Press, 1955], p. 119.) In the same volume Kaysen takes a similar line of attack, pointing to factors other than concentration which must be taken into account in order to explain product market behavior. Other contributors (George J. Stigler, Tibor Scitovsky, and William Fellner), while generally unhappy with the performance of the concentration hypothesis, tend to view it as the most promising operational device available; they generally place major emphasis on the need for improved concentration measures and more comprehensive empirical tests of these measures.

    5. See, for example, the Richard Ruggles essay (''The Nature of Price Flexibility and the Determinants of Relative Price Changes in the Economy'') in *Business Concentration and Price Policy*, pp. 441-95. See also Joe S. Bain, ''Relation of Profit Rate to Industry Concentration: American Manufacturing, 1936-1940,'' *The Quarterly Journal of Economics*, LXV, No. 3 (August, 1951), pp. 293-324; and, for a more recent effort, Victor R. Fuchs, ''Integration, Concentration, and Profits in Manufacturing Industries,'' *The Quarterly Journal of Economics*, LXXV (May, 1961), pp. 278-91.

clarification. Further words of caution concerning this aspect of the measures presented and analyzed in the following pages will not be considered necessary.

2. CONCENTRATION CURVES, CONCENTRATION RATIOS, AND A SUMMARY OF FINDINGS

In the preceding section market structure was related to monopsonistic behavior along these lines: monopsony is most likely to occur in those labor market situations in which a few firms hire a large proportion of the employed workers. The problem that is immediately encountered in the effort to make this statement operational is that of sharpening its imprecise language. How many employers are "a few"? What percentage of the employed labor force constitutes "a large proportion"?

The correct general answer to this sort of question is clear: "a few" and "a large proportion" are those numbers which lead to the best predictions of monopsonistic behavior. But little empirical work has been done by way of testing the labor market concentration hypothesis, so these numbers are not now known. The appropriate procedure, therefore, would seem to be to choose as many probably relevant measures as possible, compare them, and test them against each other. Thus the processes of testing the theory and refining the measures are interdependent. As pointed out earlier, however, testing the basic hypothesis is beyond the scope of this study; we are concerned here only with a preliminary investigation of the extent and characteristics of concentration.

Ideally, the accomplishment of this more limited aim would involve the presentation of a complete set of concentration measures for each market. This in turn would make it possible to construct a complete set of concentration curves, such as that shown in Figure 1—curves providing for each market the cumulative percentage of employment by number of employers, when all employers have been arrayed from largest to smallest.

Such a task would be a large one for most United States labor markets—and especially large for certain of those markets. For example, there were more than 100,000 firms in Cook County, Illinois, at the time of the study, and that county is only a part of the Chicago labor market area. Obtaining firm employment figures, ranking them, and computing em-

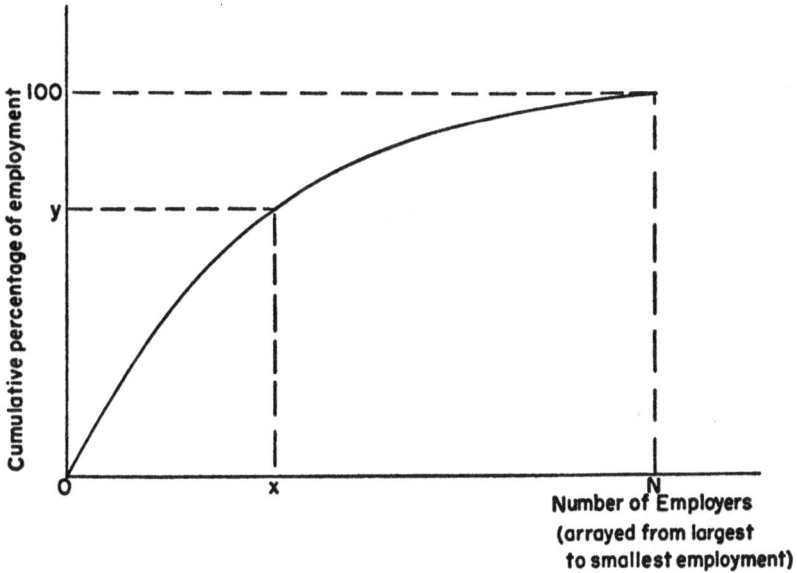

FIG. 1. The Concentration Curve

ployment percentages for all the firms in that metropolitan area would obviously be a sizable task. Thus a choice had to be made between intensive investigation of the concentration curves of a few labor markets and a less intensive examination of those of a larger number. The decision made in this connection tended in the direction of the second alternative; three points—those corresponding with the largest firm, the four largest firms, and the ten largest firms—on the concentration curves of 1774 labor market areas were estimated. It is these estimates that constitute the basic data of this study.[6]

The judgments underlying the decision to look less deeply but more broadly should be stated explicitly. First, there is the belief that ten is a fairly large number in the context of this study: that, in other words, monopsonistic behavior is unlikely to be observed unless something like ten or fewer employers hire the majority of the employees in the market. It is this belief that leads to the widespread use of the numbers three, four, and eight in product market studies. Second,

6. In addition to these, rough overestimates of a fourth point on the concentration curves—that for the thirty largest firms—were made by assuming that those firms which ranked eleven through thirty had the same number of employees as the tenth-ranking firm. These overestimates are used at several points in the study to provide a rough picture of the concentration curves beyond the point of the ten largest employers.

there is the judgment that those markets which rank high in concentration by the three measures presented here would also rank high at points beyond these on the concentration curves. There turns out to be a good deal of support for this belief in the data presented in Chapter III;[7] the same tendency has been observed in product market data.[8] Third, it was felt that the identification and ranking by degree of concentration of a large number of labor market areas has more to offer, at this stage of our understanding of monopsonistic problems, than a more detailed examination of the concentration characteristics of a few areas.

The three measures that represent the points on the concentration curves are called "concentration ratios"; for convenience they are expressed as percentages—percentages of the total employed labor force in local labor markets hired by the largest, the four largest, and the ten largest firms located in those markets. To illustrate, consider a labor market in which the largest firm has 100 employees, the three next-largest have a combined total of 150 employees, and the six next-largest firms have a combined total of 150 employees; if there are 1,000 employed workers in the labor market area altogether, the three "concentration ratios" are 10 per cent (for the single largest firm), 25 per cent (for the four largest firms), and 40 per cent (for the ten largest firms). Such percentages were computed for 1,774 local labor market areas, in which approximately 93 per cent of the total employed labor force was located.[9]

7. See especially the data of Table 6, in which the rankings of the labor markets at the three measured points are shown to be highly correlated; these rank correlation coefficients indicate a strong tendency for those labor markets showing highest concentration ratios for the single largest employer to have the highest concentration ratios for the four and ten largest employers also. More direct evidence is contained in footnote ''a'' to that table: estimates of the thirty-largest-firm ratios were found to correlate highly with the ratios for the four largest firms.

8. See Gideon Rosenbluth in *Business Concentration and Price Policy*, pp. 64-65.

9. It should be noted that it is just as reasonable to measure concentration by an alternative method, specifying the least number of firms required to account for, say, 50 per cent of the employed workers in a market. Brief reference to Table 4 will make it clear that the use of such an indicator, even for very low concentration levels of 10 or 20 per cent, would have greatly increased the computational work involved in preparing the measures. Moreover, the evidence referred to in footnote 7 above indicates that such measures would rank labor markets by concentration in much the same way as the one-four-ten largest-firms technique. Rosenbluth's experiments with distributions of firms by industry are quite interesting in this connection also; he shows, for example, high rank corre-

Brief reference was made in Section 1 to the fact that this project was made possible by the relatively recent availability of data on firm employment by geographic location. These data are a by-product of the Old-Age and Survivors Insurance program. Under law, employers covered by this legislation must make quarterly reports to the Bureau of Old-Age and Survivors Insurance; these reports provide employment and wage information upon which workers' retirement and insurance benefits are based. Tabulations based on the first of these reports of 1948, providing covered employment during the pay period ending nearest March 15 of that year, were produced by the bureau for the purpose of publishing the *1948 County Business Patterns.*[10] It was from these tabulations that the numerators of the concentration ratios were obtained.[11]

The denominators of the concentration ratios are estimates of the employed labor forces of the 1,774 labor markets. Geographically speaking, these markets were defined as single counties or small clusters of counties. The 1948 labor force estimates for these counties were made from 1940 and 1950 Census information. The estimating procedure involved the assumption that the changes in sizes of the county labor forces over the ten-year period—as shown by comparison of the two census figures—took place smoothly. That is, estimates of the 1948 labor forces for all markets were made by the "straight-line" method; for example, a county showing labor forces of 70,000 in 1940 and 80,000 in 1950 would be estimated at 78,000 for 1948. It was these estimates, adjusted for the prevailing level of unemployment, that were used as the denominators of the ratios.[12]

These ratios—measures of the relative sizes of the few largest firms in local labor markets—were used to investigate

lations between certain industries as ranked by the percentage of employment accounted for by the three largest firms and as ranked by the number of firms required to account for 80 per cent of employment. See, Rosenbluth, *Business Concentration and Price Policy*, pp. 66-69.

10. U.S. Department of Commerce, *County Business Patterns, First Quarter, 1948: Business Establishments, Employment, and Taxable Pay Rolls, By Industry Groups, Under Old-Age and Survivors Insurance Program* (Washington: U.S. Government Printing Office, 1949).

11. For a detailed description of the way these sources were used to obtain firm employment data, for estimates of errors in the procedures used, and for other shortcomings of these data, see the Appendix, Sections 1 through 6.

12. More detail on these estimating procedures and sources is provided in the Appendix, Sections 1 and 7.

the absolute level of concentration prevailing in labor markets and the relationships between concentration and the following: firm size, the size of labor markets (as measured by the number of employed workers), industrial composition of the labor force, and geographic region. The major findings of the inquiry will be briefly summarized in this same order.

1. The level of employer concentration at the time of this study was not high. Thus, the data show that the four largest firms hired more than 50 per cent of the total employed local labor force in at least 1.1 per cent but not more than 8.7 per cent of the areas studied; at least 0.3 per cent and not more than 3.7 per cent of the total employed labor force was located in these areas. Comparable percentage limits for the single largest firms in labor markets were (for areas) 0.3-2.3 and (for labor force) 0.1-0.6; for the ten largest firms the percentage limits were (for areas) 2.2-18.7 and (for labor force) 0.9-9.6.

2. Increasing concentration in local labor markets tends to be associated with increasing dominance by the largest firm of the other large firms in the market areas. Thus the largest firm employed 18.8 per cent of the sum of the employment of the ten largest firms, among the bottom-ranking (by concentration) 10 per cent of the areas, and 48.2 per cent among the top-ranking 10 per cent of the areas.

3. There is a tendency for the size of labor markets (as measured by total employment) to decrease as concentration increases. Analysis of various size categories of the areas showed that this tendency derived primarily from a marked inverse relationship among the very large and very small areas; it seemed to be nonexistent among the numerous areas of intermediate labor force size. Both the level of concentration and the inverse size-concentration relationship are consistent with an hypothesis that stresses random factors as the basic explanation of concentration. The lapse in the inverse relationship between concentration and community size, however, is inconsistent with the acceptance of this hypothesis as a complete explanation—that is, the "lapse" indicates the presence of other systematic elements in the data.

4. The investigation of the industry aspects of concentration involved analysis of the industrial composition of the labor forces of both "all firms" and "large firms only" in

concentrated areas. With respect to the analysis of the former, there was a clear tendency, among broad industry groups, for "mining" and "manufacturing" to be disproportionately represented; in concentrated areas the percentage of the labor force allocated to these two industry groups was approximately twice as great as in comparable non-concentrated areas.

The labor force of the *largest firms* in high concentration areas was also disproportionately allocated among industries. Nine industries accounted for 88 per cent of the total employment of the 100 top-ranking firms in the 100 areas of highest concentration; these same nine industries accounted for only 25.8 per cent of the United States total covered (by OASI) employment in 1948. They are (using a finer industry classification system than in the paragraph above): "mining," "textile mill products," "lumber and wood products," "paper and allied products," "chemicals and allied products," "primary metal industries," "machinery, except electrical," "electrical machinery," and "transportation equipment."

These industries had at least this one characteristic in common: they contained disproportionate shares of large firms. They accounted for only 4.8 per cent of the *total* number of "covered" firms, whereas their percentage of "covered" *large* firms (500 employees and over) was 44. Thus it is not surprising that these same industries accounted for disproportionate percentages of the labor forces of the largest firms in non-concentrated areas as well as in concentrated areas—65 per cent, as opposed to 88 per cent (mentioned above) for the high concentration areas.

The importance of the nine industries varied with the size of labor markets. To illustrate: "mining" was relatively more important in small labor markets than in large, "transportation equipment" was more important among large markets than small, and "textiles" showed up as an important industry among labor market areas of all sizes.

5. The data showed concentration to have strong regional characteristics. For example, in a ranking of all labor market areas by concentration, 40 per cent of the labor force of the East South Central region, as compared with only 4 per cent of that of the Pacific region, was contained in areas ranking above the median. Regional variation in concentra-

tion seemed to be explainable in terms of industry and community size; that is, regions ranking high in concentration tended to be those containing the nine high concentration industries in effective combination with numerous relatively small labor market areas. There was no evidence of systematic variation that could be imputed to region alone—or to other factors.

The findings listed above have been stated without qualification, as if there were no question about the accuracy of the data from which the indexes of concentration were obtained or whether they measure what ought to be measured. In fact, there are serious problems at the conceptual and operational levels involving both the preparation and interpretation of the ratios; these issues are discussed in detail in the following chapter and in the Appendix. The "errors" involved in the concentration indexes generally appear to be such as to cancel themselves out—very roughly speaking—insofar as their aggregate effect on the absolute level of concentration is concerned. This statement, however, is based on the assumption that governments and non-profit firms should not be thought of in the same context with profit-oriented employers, who presumably are trying to extract monopsonistic gains from the labor market. If this assumption is dropped and if all units of government (except education) at all levels (federal, state, and local) are considered as a single "firm," concentration rises substantially. The aggregate increase from all sources of error may be as great as 72 per cent for certain of the concentration measures.

It is worth noting, however, that the acceptance of even this drastic estimate of the average error in the measures is consistent with an appraisal of the general level of concentration as being quite low. An increase in all ratios of 72 per cent would put less than 16 per cent (perhaps as little as 5 per cent) of the employed labor force in labor markets in which the four largest firms hire as much as 50 per cent of the labor force.

Chapter II

PROBLEMS IN THE MEASUREMENT OF
CONCENTRATION IN LABOR MARKETS

1. The Appropriate Definition of a Labor Market

The problem of appropriately defining labor markets for the measurement of concentration in a context relating concentration to labor monopsony has two different dimensions. The first is that of classifying labor services by type of "occupation"; the second is that of determining the geographic extent of each market. These logically separable dimensions of the problem will be considered in turn.

The following examples will illustrate the issues involved in the classification of labor by "occupation." First, suppose that the classification scheme were to put into separate classes "residential janitors" on the one hand and "non-residential janitors" on the other. It seems reasonable to suppose that being "residential" rather than "non-residential" would make little difference to janitors if the real wage rates in these two "occupations" were the same. If this supposition were correct, residential janitors could protect themselves against monopsonistic behavior among residential janitor employers by shifting to non-residential employers. This example illustrates the general proposition: all "occupations" among which there is a high degree of substitutability—easy and willing transfer among suppliers of labor—should be combined.

As a first, and admittedly rough, approximation to the truth it seems reasonable to suppose that even in the short run there is a relatively high degree of substitutability in supply among most unskilled and semi-skilled occupations; hence, no effort has been made in this study to separate these "not-skilled" occupations from each other.

Consider now a second example in which janitors are put in one class and doctors in a second. Three obvious considerations bear on such a scheme of classification: janitors generally cannot stop selling janitor services and start selling medical services in the short run; doctors generally would not want to stop selling medical services and start selling janitor services; and buyers of these two types of services would generally be expected to find them poor substitutes for each other. In a word, little interrelationship is to be expected between these markets from either the supply or demand side. This being the case, a group of employers of doctors may be able to monopsonize successfully the services of doctors without including in the group any large employers of janitors—and, of course, the same line of reasoning applies to the monopsonizing efforts of the employers of janitors. It follows that if the two occupations are treated as one, the resulting concentration curve may differ significantly from the relevant concentration curves for the two separate occupations.

The fact that the skilled occupations in the short run tend to be non-competing with the not-skilled occupations and with each other made it desirable to limit the scope of this study to the not-skilled occupations taken as a single group. The impossibility of obtaining occupational breakdowns of the BOASI firm employment figures acted as a powerful force in the same direction. Within this more restricted range of study, it would clearly have been preferable, given the present imperfect understanding of inter-occupational labor mobility, to prepare concentration curves for each of several different occupational definitions of the not-skilled. But, again, this was impossible because of the lack of firm-level occupational information. Instead, a plan was adopted that was designed to bracket the real-world, not-skilled ratio in each market by providing a pair of measures for each of the three points on the concentration curves, one of which tended to be "too small" and the other of which tended to be "too large."

Thus, in the next chapter two sets of estimates of the concentration ratios are given. The first set, called "Overall-1," "Overall-4," and "Overall-10," includes employees in all occupations in both numerators and denominators: for example, the Overall concentration ratio for the single largest firm ("Overall-1") has as its numerator the total employment of the largest firm in the area and, as its denominator, the total employed labor force of the market area.

These Overall estimates probably are unreliable measures of the extent of concentration for particular *skilled* occupations. To illustrate, suppose that the largest firm in a certain labor market hires 25 per cent of the market's total labor force and, at the same time, is the *only* employer of a particular kind of highly skilled labor; under these circumstances, the Overall-1 concentration ratio is an entirely misleading indicator of the concentration situation in the market for that particular skilled component of the local labor force.

If, however, the employment in skilled occupations *as a group* tends to be distributed more or less proportionately throughout all firms, concentration ratios computed from data covering all occupations will tend to give a reasonably accurate reflection of the extent of concentration that obtains in the *not-skilled* labor market. To continue the illustration of the preceding paragraph: if all firms in the market hire the same proportion of skilled workers, the figure "25" will accurately reflect the percentages of the market's not-skilled workers hired by the largest firm.

As a matter of fact, there is a bias in the distribution of skilled workers (as a group) by firm size: it is in the direction of small firms. Since skilled workers tend to constitute a larger proportion of the employment of small firms than of large firms (alternatively, since not-skilled workers are distributed disproportionately toward large firms), there is a strong presumption that Overall ratios *understate* the actual concentration situation in the not-skilled labor market. The extent of this tendency toward understatement was estimated, by a rather crude technique, to be approximately 16 per cent.[1]

The second set of estimates was prepared by adjusting the first set: skilled workers were deducted from the denominators of the three Overall ratios; the numerators were not changed. The resulting ratios, called "Maximum-1," "Maximum-4," and "Maximum-10," must be greater than the "true" not-skilled ratios of the mid-March, 1948, markets if the top-ranking firms in those markets hired any skilled

1. The analysis underlying this estimate used BOASI and census data to indicate (a) that certain industries contain disproportionately large percentages of large firms and (b) that these same industries contain disproportionately large percentages of not-skilled workers. See Section 8 of the Appendix.

workers at all.[2] The belief that they probably do represent an overstatement of the degree of concentration among the not-skilled occupations is supported by the fact that Maximum concentration ratios well over 100 per cent were found for the largest *single* firm in some markets.

For the United States as a whole in 1950, the excluded skilled occupations as defined for purposes of computing Maximum concentration ratios[3] included 43.5 per cent of the labor force in all occupations. If the "skilled" workers were distributed proportionately among all labor markets, all Maximum concentration ratios would be approximately 77 per cent larger than their Overall counterparts. Thus the two sets of estimates probably bracket the "true" concentration ratios for the not-skilled occupations taken as a group, as far as the skill or labor classification problem is concerned. In terms of concentration curves, the "real" not-skilled curves would generally be expected to lie be-

2. This statement obviously assumes the validity of the procedures by which the numerators and denominators were originally estimated.

3. The denominators of the Maximum estimates were obtained from the Overall denominators in the following manner:

1. For each labor market studied in this paper two figures were obtained from census labor force data for 1950:

    a. the total employed labor force in all occupations, as follows:

        (1) *Professional, technical, and kindred workers
        (2) *Farmers and farm managers
        (3) *Managers, officials, and proprietors, except farm
        (4) Clerical and kindred workers
        (5) Sales workers
        (6) *Craftsmen, foremen, and kindred workers
        (7) Operatives and kindred workers
        (8) Private household workers
        (9) Service workers, except private household
      (10) *Farm laborers, unpaid family workers
      (11) *Farm laborers, except unpaid, and farm foremen
      (12) Laborers, except farm and mine
      (13) Occupation not reported

    b. the total employed labor force in all occupations (a) less that part of it in the occupational classes designated above by asterisks.

2. It was then assumed that the ratio of (b) to (a) would differ little from the corresponding ratio for 1948. Thus the denominators of the Overall concentration ratios were multiplied by the corresponding ratios of (b) to (a) to obtain the denominators of the Maximum concentration ratios.

The primary source of 1950 Census data used for this operation and for many other purposes throughout this study was Table 43, "Economic Characteristics of the Population, by Sex, for Counties: 1950" (U.S. Bureau of the Census, *United States Census of Population: 1950. General Characteristics*, Population Census Reports, P-B Series, Preprints of Volume II, Chapter B [Washington: U.S. Government Printing Office, 1952]).

tween the Maximum curves and the Overall curves, considerably closer to the latter.

It will be noted that two of the excluded occupational groups indicated in footnote 3—unpaid family farm laborers and paid farm laborers and foremen—are not skilled workers. These exclusions were made in deference to the widespread view that there is not high substitutability in supply between farm and non-farm not-skilled occupations. There is a good deal of evidence, both on mobility and on wages, to suggest that this view is wrong—except perhaps in certain parts of the South. To the extent that it is wrong, the denominators of the Maximum estimates are too low and the concentration ratios figured from them are too high. It was estimated, on the assumption that these agricultural workers were proportionately distributed among *all* areas, that their inclusion in Maximum denominators would have decreased these ratios by an average of about 7 per cent. Specific investigation of *high* concentration areas on a sample basis showed that these areas tended to have slightly larger proportions of agricultural workers; the inclusion of agricultural workers in their denominators would have lowered their Maximum concentration ratios by approximately 11 per cent.[4]

There are, of course, many other criteria in addition to skill by which labor may be classified: sex, race, color of eyes, etc. Are such criteria relevant? Would it be desirable, for purposes of measuring concentration, to compute separate ratios for, say, "blue-eyed" and "not-blue-eyed" workers? There certainly is little substitutability in supply between these two groups, so this basis of classification admirably meets the cross-elasticity of supply test for separate treatment. The scheme of classification fails, however, to meet the second test: low cross-elasticity of demand. For surely most employers will act as though the two classes of workers were excellent substitutes for each other. It is, in fact, a matter of common observation that there are large areas within the not-skilled labor market for which high cross-elasticity of demand obtains—across such lines of demarcation as color of eyes, sex, and race. It is this characteristic

4. The process of putting the agricultural workers back into the denominators of the high concentration areas had little effect upon their relative concentration positions. (More details concerning the above estimates of the effects of deleting agricultural workers from the denominators of Maximum concentration ratios may be found in Section 8 of the Appendix.)

of the market that makes such criteria generally irrelevant for purposes of this study.

Consider now the second dimension of a labor market: its geographic extent. Properly delineating the labor markets for not-skilled workers at a given wage level involves drawing lines, around the smallest possible areas, which (lines) simultaneously (a) put "most" of the potential labor supply of the inclosed firms within the same boundaries as those firms, and (b) include "most" of the firms that the inclosed workers think of as excellent substitutes within the same boundaries as those workers. It is difficult to believe that many economists would seriously argue that city blocks meet these requirements; surely they are much too small. On the other hand, most surely *would* argue that considering the whole United States as a single, not-skilled labor market also misses the mark. It is much too large. For any reasonably defined short-run period, an employer of not-skilled labor in California will not be viewed by workers residing in New York as a good substitute for New York employers.

In the absence of generally-agreed-upon information on the elasticity of supply of labor to spatially separated groups of employers there is some virtue in taking a conservative view—one that probably subdivides employers into too many groups, or labor markets, rather than too few. Although this procedure tends to overstate the extent of concentration, it makes it more convenient for those who believe that the groups are too small to regroup them according to their own criteria.

As a matter of fact, the BOASI data place a lower limit on the size of area that can be considered, for these data are classified geographically by county. There are approximately 3,100 counties in the United States varying in size from a few square miles to some very large counties of approximately 20,000 square miles. More than 90 per cent of the counties, however, have an area of less than 2,000 square miles. Thus most of them are so small that daily commuting of employees in one place in a county to employment at another place in the same county is relatively easy.[5] For this reason it was felt that counties typically would not be too *large* to be considered labor markets. Indeed, in a

5. A circle twenty-five miles in radius has an area of approximately 2,000 square miles.

number of cases, it was quite apparent that the county was an inappropriate unit because it was too small: comparison of BOASI data (which placed workers in the county of their employment) with census data (in which workers were located by county of residence), indicated that many employees were commuting across county lines. To meet this problem, population concentrations in all counties used in the study were checked; in those cases in which a relatively large commuting flow appeared likely, two or more counties were combined for purposes of making the concentration measurements.[6]

About one-third of the counties in the United States included no establishments subject to Old-Age and Survivors Insurance coverage that employed as many as 100 workers in 1948. Characteristically these were sparsely populated areas, so it was decided to exclude all such counties from the study. The labor force of these excluded areas comprised less than 7 per cent of the total United States labor force,[7] so a substantial reduction in the amount of computational effort was achieved at very little cost in terms of labor force coverage.[8] After these exclusions and after the combination of some counties into single labor market areas, there were 1,774 areas, each considered a "labor market" area, for which concentration ratios were computed.[9]

6. "Standard metropolitan areas" as defined by the census were used in this study as single labor market areas. Since these census definitions were designed to solve precisely the sort of problem under consideration here, it is reasonable to assume that their use reduced the magnitude of possible commuting error to acceptable levels, except for those occasional situations in which a medium or small-sized city lay quite close to a county line. A county-by-county search revealed twenty-three such situations; this necessitated the combination of forty-six non-metropolitan counties into twenty-three single labor market areas. Altogether, sixty-eight multi-county labor market areas were formed for the purpose of reducing commuting error in concentration ratios.

7. More exactly, the total 1950 civilian labor force of the omitted areas was slightly greater than 3.7 million, which was 6.3 per cent of the national total of about 59 million. The five highest-ranking states, in terms of omitted civilian labor force, were these: Iowa, Kansas, Nebraska, Oklahoma, and Mississippi.

8. The arithmetic mean of the employment in the largest firms in the twenty-five highest-ranking areas (according to Maximum-1 concentration ratios) was slightly in excess of 3700 employees. Thus it seems that the biggest firms in high concentration areas tend to be quite large in absolute terms. It would appear to be improbable, therefore, that the deletions mentioned in the text above caused many high concentration areas to be missed.

9. Section 9 of the Appendix contains a detailed discussion of the several problems that arose in connection with the geographic delineation of the labor markets.

2. TRANSITORY ELEMENTS IN THE CLASSIFICATION OF FIRMS BY EMPLOYMENT IN MARCH, 1948[10]

The concentration measures presented in this study are based on a classification of employers by the size of their employment in mid-March, 1948. Suppose that in a particular labor market the largest (one, four, ten) firms were subject to seasonal, cyclical, or trend factors that were not the same for them as for the other firms in the market. Then if the concentration measures were computed from data unadjusted for these factors, these measures also would contain seasonal, cyclical, or trend components. In this study, the basic employment data were not adjusted for these factors— the data for such adjustments did not exist. Thus it may very well be true that the estimates of concentration for March, 1948, would not be the same as those for some other month in 1948 or in another year.

The preceding sentence, though correct, nevertheless is misleading if it is read to imply that (apart from other defects in the data) the concentration ratios based on the classification of employers by their employment in March, 1948, are the relevant ratios *for that date*. Consider the following hypothetical example: in a particular labor market the ten largest firms according to March, 1948, data accounted for 50 per cent of the total employment in the market. Therefore, the concentration ratio for the ten largest firms in March, 1948, on this method of classifying firms by size was 50 per cent. This same procedure was applied to the data of all months in the six-year period centered on March, 1948, and the concentration ratio for *all* of these months was 50 per cent. It was not true, however, that the ten firms having the largest employment in March, 1948, also had the largest employment in every other month of the six-year period. Indeed, over the six-year period twenty different firms appeared at least once among the top ten. Thus though in each month of the period the ten largest firms, measured by that month's employment data, employed 50 per cent of the employment in the area, the ten firms *whose average employment over the six-year period* was largest must have employed less than 50 per cent of the total employment on the

10. For discussions of the conceptual problem of this section as it relates to concentration in product markets, see Stigler and Rosenbluth in *Business Concentration and Price Policy,* pp. 5-6 and 92-94, respectively.

average. To put it another way: if the firms had been classified on the basis of their average employment over the six-year period, the number of firms employing on the average 50 per cent of the total employment must have exceeded ten.

The theory relating concentration to monopsony, given briefly in Chapter I, stated that monopsony was more likely where concentration was high than where it was low because, in general, (a) collective action is necessary to capture monopsonistic gains and (b) such collective action is more costly the lower the concentration of employment among employers. It is clearly inconsistent to argue both that organization for collective action tends to be costly and also that organization easily can accommodate itself to changes from one month to another in the list of its membership. Thus the concentration curve that is relevant for March, 1948, is not the curve based on the classification of employers by their employment in that month but the curve based on the classification of employers by the more or less "permanent" size of their employment.[11]

Unfortunately employer size distribution data comparable with those provided by the BOASI for March, 1948, but averaging employment over a longer period are not available. Thus it is impossible to know with precision the extent to which the concentration ratios presented in this paper overestimate those based on data classifying employers by employment averaged over a period substantially longer than a month. However, one of the basic sources used in this study did provide employment data for firms hiring 100 or more workers for mid-March, 1947, as well as for mid-March, 1948. This made it possible to conduct two types of experiments that provide some insight into the dimensions of the transitory problem. Three samples were used in these experiments: one twenty-eight area sample with a low concentration bias; one thirty-two area general random sample; and one consisting of the twenty-five high-

11. The preceding discussion leads naturally to the question: What is the correct length of the period over which employment should be averaged (and, indeed, what kind of average should be used?) in classifying firms by the size of their employment? The methodological issue that these questions raise has been dealt with previously. Here the treatment must be the same; the length of the period and the method of averaging that are "correct" are those that predict monopsony best.

est-ranking areas, according to Maximum-1 concentration ratios.

The first of the experiments was an effort to measure the extent to which changes among the top-ranking firms in labor markets take place. All three samples showed essentially the same thing: as many as 25 per cent of the firms that occupied a rank position among the top four firms in 1948 may have occupied a lower rank in 1947.[12] This result indicates that the transitory problem is probably an important one, but it does little to show the magnitude of error involved.

The second experiment consisted of an attempt at direct measurement of the effect upon concentration ratios of transitory elements in the data. This was done in the following fashion: for each labor market area concentration ratios were computed separately for 1947 and 1948, and these ratios were averaged; the result was a set of ratios from which the transitory effects had not been removed. Next, a new set of ratios was constructed by averaging the employment of the firms in each area for the two mid-March dates, ranking these average employment figures within each area, and computing new concentration ratios by dividing, e.g., the largest of these averages by the average employed labor force. This second set of ratios will tend to be smaller than the first in those areas in which rank mobility has occurred among the largest firms. "Transitory differentials" were computed by expressing the difference between these two types of ratios as a percentage of the first.

The averages of these differentials for the sample with the low concentration bias and that for the general random sample were both about 6 per cent; the average of those for the high concentration areas was approximately 10 per cent.[13]

The above estimates do not, of course, reflect any seasonal influences, since they are based on two seasonally-identical points in time. Rough estimates of the impact of seasonal variations in employment can be inferred, however, from other

12. Rosenbluth provides highly comparable product market data. He shows that two or more of the four leading firms were replaced by other firms between 1935 and 1937 in 40 per cent of the (262) products investigated. See Rosenbluth in *Business Concentration and Price Policy*, p. 93.

13. The rank correlation coefficient for the high concentration sample areas as ranked by the two types of average concentration ratios was +.74.

The two experiments described in the text above were designed with the aim of not understating the magnitude of the problem. The details of the experiments, as provided in Section 10 of the Appendix, suggest overstatement.

data. For the major employment change of this type is the rapid rise in aggregate employment throughout the spring and summer associated with the increase in construction and agricultural activity; as employment in these industries begins to decrease from the late summer peak, increases in retail trade employment tends to slow the aggregate decline. With the post-Christmas let-up in retail trade, the seasonal low in aggregate employment is reached.

Most of the seasonal employment changes take place in industries characterized by small firms. Thus, seasonality probably will tend to have little impact upon the numerators of concentration ratios; denominators, however, will tend to move with the seasonal pattern. The major effect of this transitory factor, then, is surely to cause concentration ratios to fall from mid-winter to late-summer and then to rise slowly back to the mid-winter high. It was estimated that compensating for this factor would lower the mid-March, 1948, concentration ratios by 2 or 3 per cent, on the average. Since the agricultural component of seasonal employment is by far the largest, since agriculture tends to be located in small (employment) areas, and since concentration tends to be greatest in small areas, the impact of seasonal factors is probably slightly greater in high concentration areas.[14]

The data are sketchy. They indicate, however, that the problem posed by transitory elements in the data is a real one; and they suggest that, if mid-March data were available for a period of several years, concentration ratios based upon some sort of average ("stabilized") mid-March employment figures over various "long" intervals would be smaller than comparable "long" interval averages of concentration ratios computed independently for each mid-March period. The seasonal factor seems to be such that the average ("stabilized") mid-March concentration ratios, in turn, would tend to be greater than ratios computed on the basis of employment data averaged over all months throughout the several-year interval. Rough estimates of the extent of overstatement for the one-year interval discussed above suggest that a maximum due to non-seasonal transitory factors is 6 per cent for most of the areas and 10 per cent for those of very high concentration.[15] The seasonal estimate is less satisfactory,

14. Additional details concerning the seasonal estimates may be found in the Appendix, Section 10.

15. This estimate may strictly be applied only to the single largest firm concen-

but it probably averages around 2 or 3 per cent for most areas with a tendency to be somewhat larger in areas of high concentration.

3. THE RELEVANT EMPLOYING UNIT

Thus far the terms "employer" and "firm" have been used as if they referred in a clean, clear-cut fashion to certain economic units. This is not the case, however, so the ambiguities surrounding the terms must be examined. The first of these concerns the question, what to do about "firms" that are not profit-oriented? Would such employers (governments and non-profit firms) typically be expected to engage in collusive action with other employers with the aim of depressing wages? The other source of uncertainty derives from the fact that several establishments of the same firm may be located in the same local labor market area: should they or should they not be combined for purposes of this study? Do they typically act individually or collectively in the market for the services of labor?

The proper way to answer such questions as these has already been suggested in several different contexts: the operational definitions that "work best" (i.e., predict monopsonistic behavior most successfully) are the ones to be used. When a choice among untested alternatives must be made, proper procedure involves (data permitting) the adoption of definitions for which the best case can be made, the provision of estimates relating the chosen definition to next-best alternatives, and the presentation of basic data in such a way that other investigators can conveniently modify them according to their own preferences.

Government and non-profit firms were not subject to Old-Age and Survivors Insurance in 1948; this fact, strongly reinforced by the judgment that most students of the labor market do not think of such "firms" as monopsonists, made it desirable to "solve" this aspect of the definitional problem by excluding these employers from the numerators of concentration ratios. And so the data presented and analyzed in Chapter III may be thought of as being predicated on the "assumption" that these types of "firms" never engage in

---

tration ratios. Such data as were available indicated that four-firm concentration ratio adjustments would not differ much. The only basis for applying these results to the ten-firm ratios is the tentative similarity between the one- and four-firm estimates.

monopsonistic activity. In Section 5 of this chapter a crude effort is made to indicate the magnitude of the increase in the concentration measures that would be brought about by dropping this "assumption."

The attack on the other employer-ambiguity problem— what to do with two or more establishments of the same firm in the same local labor market area—must be launched from a less elegant position: the OASI data are not completely on an establishment nor firm basis. The Bureau encourages establishment reporting—reporting on a single unit, single business activity, basis. By 1948 most employers had accepted the Bureau's preferences in this regard, but some—predominantly in industries such as retail trade where a single firm might have several small units in the same county—had not.[16]

Ideally, the data should be put entirely on an establishment basis; the resulting concentration ratios should then be supplemented with estimates of the effect of converting the data to a firm basis. For the reason mentioned in the preceding paragraph the data could be moved no farther in the direction of being put on an establishment basis; this was not crucial since they were already quite close to this position. It was possible to obtain reasonably good estimates of the increase in the concentration ratios associated with putting the data uniformly on a firm basis. Data sources (a) permitted the identification of establishments hiring 100 or more workers who were part of a multi-unit firm, and (b) provided supplementary locational information that made it possible to see if two or more establishments in the same firm were located in the same labor market area.

The thirty-two area general random sample and the sample of twenty-five high concentration areas were used in this "firm-establishment" investigation.[17] Firms hiring 100 or more workers in all of these areas were scrutinized; where two or more establishments of the same firm were found in the same labor market area, they were combined; the resulting "firms" were ranked and concentration ratios were recomputed; for each area, the difference between firm and establishment concentration ratios was expressed as a percentage of the establishment ratios. For the thirty-two area sample

16. U.S. Department of Commerce, *1948 County Business Patterns*, Part I, p. 5.
17. Both of these samples were used in the investigation of transitory elements in the data. See the preceding section of this chapter.

the averages of these percentage differentials were as follows: for the single largest employer, 3.40 per cent; for the four largest employers, 1.75 per cent; and for the ten largest employers, 1.01 per cent. For the twenty-five area sample they were, respectively, 3.86, 0.51, and 0.22 per cent.

The sample areas were ranked according to the original single-largest firm concentration ratios and again according to these same ratios after they had been revised. The Spearman rank correlation coefficient was +.9857 for the thirty-two area sample and +.9092 for the twenty-five area sample.

These investigations suggest that the following tentative generalizations are not extreme:

1. If the concentration ratios of this study were all put completely on a firm basis, the general level of concentration would rise only slightly above the level of the unadjusted ratios—the rise would probably be less than 5 per cent.

2. The concentration ratios of most of the areas would be unaffected by the adjustment: most of the areas are already largely on a firm concentration ratio basis.

3. The process of putting the data uniformly on a firm basis would bring about little rearrangement in the rank positions of labor market areas.

There will be no attempt in the following pages of this study to distinguish among establishments, combinations of establishments in the same area, and firms. The term "firm" will be used throughout to refer to the business organizations that report as a unit to the BOASI.[18]

4. The Relevant Unit for Measuring Employment

This study represents an attempt to select out the firms that exercise the greatest impact upon the not-skilled portion of local labor markets and to state their influence quantitatively, by means of indexes of concentration. The basic data of the study consist of ratios of large firm employments to total employed labor force in each area. The problem under investigation in this section is that of discovering to what extent the concentration situation as shown by the number of employed workers as of mid-March, 1948 is different from

18. Additional details of the procedure followed in computing firm concentration ratios and more information tending to support the three concluding generalizations in the text are provided in the Appendix, Section 11.

what it would have been if some other indicator of labor market impact had been used.

BOASI data are available that permit some estimate of the extent to which *employment* concentration ratios diverge from concentration ratios based on *payrolls*. For firms with 100 or more employees, total first quarter payrolls (January through March, 1948), are available; in addition, total first quarter payrolls for *all* covered units in each county can be obtained from the *County Business Patterns* bulletins. Thus it is possible to compute wages paid in the three-month period to the employees of large units as a percentage of total wages paid in covered employment (for the same three-month period) in each area. The resulting concentration ratios are highly comparable with employment concentration ratios in which BOASI covered-employment data are used for *both* numerators and denominators; these latter concentration ratios may be prepared by substituting the *total covered employment* of each labor market area—again, as presented in the *County Business Patterns* bulletins—for the census-derived denominators in the ratios used throughout this study. A difference in these types of ratios is that one, the set of payroll ratios, represents average concentration over a three-month interval whereas the other, the set of employment ratios, represents the concentration situation as it existed during the pay period ending nearest March 15.

Concentration ratios of these two types were computed for the two samples used in the preceding section: the thirty-two area random sample and the twenty-five area sample of very high concentration areas. In almost all of these areas payroll concentration ratios exceeded employment concentration ratios. So, individual area percentage differentials were computed by subtracting the employment ratios from payroll ratios and expressing the difference as a percentage of the former. Simple arithmetic means of these differentials (based on single-largest-firm concentration ratios) were 27 per cent, for the thirty-two area sample, and 12 per cent, for the twenty-five area sample.

Two questions must be raised in evaluating these results. The first has to do with the reality of the difference: the exclusion of self-employed workers from BOASI data tends to produce payroll concentration ratios that are larger than employment concentration ratios,[19] and the question is whether this factor is a complete explanation of the observed differential. Upon investigation, it appeared likely that only part of the difference between payroll and employment ratios was to be explained in this fashion and that, therefore, a genuine differential existed, i.e., large firms in labor markets tend to pay higher wages.

The second question concerns the meaningfulness of the differential in regard to the measurement of concentration: is the differential a premium paid out of necessity by the large firm to compensate for non-monetary disadvantages that workers attribute to its size, or is it a premium that serves the function of attracting workers of higher quality to the large firm? If it is in fact compensation for undesirable aspects of large-firm employment the differential clearly tends to cause overstatement of the absolute level of concentration, so that the *employment* ratios more accurately reflect the "true" level.

But what if the explanation of the differential lies in the fact that large firms purchase "better" (i.e., more productive than average) labor? For certain analytical purposes, it is appropriate to treat the purchase of "more productive than average" labor as if it were the purchase of "more units of average productivity" labor. If this is proper treatment for analysis of labor market concentration, then the differentials are meaningful and the employment ratios are *less* accurate than the payroll ratios. It may well be that this is not proper analytical procedure, however. For purposes of indicating the costliness or difficulty of employer collusion, minor qualitative differences among the not-skilled types of labor purchased by the would-be monopsonists are unimportant, so that a measure which indicates only the *number* of workers— rather than one which reflects both number and quality—is more appropriate. This, of course, would mean that the employment measures are more accurate indicators of the absolute level of concentration than the payroll measures.

The problem discussed immediately above is of the same

19. The self-employed tend to be distributed primarily toward small business units; "lifting" them out of the two all-BOASI types of concentration ratios affects the denominators but, essentially, not the numerators. The impact upon the payroll denominators is greater than upon the employment denominators; e.g., removing the doctor and his income from the data for his four-person firm decreases employment of the firm by one-fourth but "wages paid" by substantially more than one-fourth.

sort as certain others previously encountered in that only success-in-prediction tests will provide a conclusive solution. All that can be said at present is that payroll concentration ratios tend to exceed employment concentration ratios by an amount that is related to the level of concentration; but present understandings of labor market phenomena do not permit the use of payroll ratios as a check upon the validity and accuracy of the absolute level of the employment ratios.

Rank correlation coefficients, reflecting the degree of similarity in rankings of areas by employment and payroll concentration ratios, were computed for the two samples. Both were high: +.9348 for the thirty-two area sample and +.9408 for the twenty-five area sample. Thus, for concentration problems in which the relative rank position of labor market areas is crucial, choosing between employment and payroll measures does not appear to be a matter of great significance—the results would be about the same in either case.

5. FIRMS NOT COVERED BY OLD-AGE AND SURVIVORS INSURANCE

The numerators of the concentration ratios used in this study were derived from OASI tabulations, which were based upon the reports of employers to the Bureau concerning their operations for the first quarter of 1948. It is the purpose of this section to return to a possible source of error, mentioned in Section 3, which grows out of the coverage limitations of the OASI legislation in 1948. Certain types of employers were specifically excluded; this means that the numerators of some—perhaps many—concentration ratios are too small. (Since the denominators were obtained from census sources, they are not affected.)

A preliminary notion of the magnitude of this problem may be obtained from these summary estimates: in 1948 the total employed labor force was approximately 59.3 million workers; of these, approximately 24 million (40.5 per cent) were not employed by firms subject to Old-Age and Survivors Insurance coverage.[20]

These figures may be seriously misleading if they are interpreted to mean that approximately four out of every ten employers who should have been included in the numerators of concentration ratios were "missed" in the data-gathering

20. "Employment Covered by Social Insurance," *Social Security Bulletin* (August, 1949), p. 20.

TABLE 1

ESTIMATED EMPLOYMENT IN AN AVERAGE WEEK IN INDUSTRIES
NOT COVERED BY OLD-AGE AND SURVIVORS INSURANCE, 1948[a]

Industry	Employment (mil.)
Railroad	1.6
Government	5.3
Agriculture	7.9
Non-agricultural self-employed	6.1
Domestic service	1.7
Other[b]	1.4
Total	24.0

[a] Source: "Employment Covered by Social Insurance," *Social Security Bulletin*, August, 1949, p. 20.
[b] Approximately one million of these are employees of non-profit organizations—charitable, educational, and religious; see U.S. Congress, Senate Committee on Finance, *Old-Age and Survivors Insurance*, 80th Cong., 2nd Sess., Senate Doc. 149, p. 18. The other 400,000 employees are casual laborers, certain fishing crew members, employees of foreign governments, etc.; see U.S., Federal Security Agency, *Compilation of the Social Security Laws, Including the Social Security Act, As Amended, and Related Enactments through July 1, 1948* (Washington: U.S. Government Printing Office, 1948), pp. 19-22.

process. Table 1 indicates that such an interpretation would probably grossly overstate the magnitude of the problem. Nevertheless, the size of the excluded labor force is indeed quite large—large enough, certainly, to make mandatory some estimation of the extent to which numerators are smaller than they should be.

It is clear that certain of the categories of Table 1 can be dismissed almost immediately as sources of difficulty—i.e., as categories containing some significant number of "large" employers of labor which should be included in the numerators of concentration ratios. Surely agriculture, for example, is predominantly an industry of small firms, so that only rarely would an agricultural employer be among the largest employers of the labor market areas studied. (It is relevant to recall that approximately one-third of all United States counties—generally speaking, the smallest ones—are not included within the scope of this study.) The same sort of reasoning applies to the non-agricultural self-employed, to domestic service, and, it seems reasonably certain, to most of the 400,000 workers in the catch-all category "Other" who are not employed by non-profit firms. All told, these small-firm employees account for 16.1 million, or about two-thirds, of the total of 24.0 million excluded workers. The fact that the basic concentration ratios tend generally to include these workers in the census-derived denominators (to the extent that they are in the 1,774 areas studied) but to exclude them from the BOASI-derived numerators cannot be a serious source of error in the data.

The remaining categories relate to types of employers that cannot be dismissed so easily. They are railroads, governments, and non-profit organizations, and together they accounted for about eight million employed workers in 1948. It is a matter of common observation that these employers sometimes are among the largest, so failure to include them in the numerators possibly could cause the extent of concentration to be understated. Unfortunately, however, there are no accessible data on the size distribution of governmental, non-profit, or railroad employing units by county in the United States. Therefore a crude adjustment procedure was devised and, according to the pattern of investigation established in earlier sections of this chapter, applied to sample data.

A conceptual line can be drawn that separates one of these types of employers, railroads, from the other two. The basis of the distinction was briefly discussed earlier, in Section 3 of this chapter; it has to do with the questionable appropriateness of including governments and non-profit firms among private, profit-seeking business enterprises in a monopsonistic context. There is, of course, no question in this regard with respect to railroad firms. The practical consequence of drawing this conceptual dividing line was that the adjustments to the sample data were made separately, for the railroads first, and then for the railroads plus governments and non-profit firms.

In these tests two samples of areas were used: the thirty-two area general random sample (used in the preceding three sections) and the twenty-five area, high-concentration sample drawn for the purpose of estimating possible error associated with the exclusion of agricultural unskilled workers from Maximum denominators (see Section 1 of this chapter). Within each labor market area of these samples, the total number of employed railroad workers was estimated for 1948 from census sources; for adjustment purposes, this total was accepted as the mid-March employment of a single railroad firm, which was then included within the rankings of large firms. When the total of employed railroad workers was such as to make this "firm" one of the ten largest, concentration ratios were recomputed as necessary. For each area individual percentage differentials were computed for the six measures: for example, the Overall-10 concentration ratio as it stood before inclusion of the railroad firm was deducted from that ratio as it was computed with the railroad firm included in the numerator in its proper rank position, and this difference was expressed as a percentage of the "unadjusted" Overall-10 concentration ratio.

The changes brought about by these sample calculations may be summarized as follows: average increases of slightly more than 6 per cent for most single-largest firm ratios, with a decline in this increase to zero for high-concentration areas; average increases of less than 13 per cent for most four-largest firm ratios, with a decline to about 2 per cent in this increase in high-concentration areas; and average increases of less than 13 per cent for most ten-largest firm ratios, with a decline to about 4 per cent for high-concentration areas.

If it is correct that the theory of monopsony is an appropriate analytical tool only for the private, profit-seeking sector of the economy, then government and private non-profit organizations, however great their relative size as employers, should not be taken into account in this study. For those who hold this view, the above estimates of the effects of including railroads in the numerators of concentration ratios constitute all that need be said about the problem of employers excluded from OASI coverage.

However, the notion that government and non-profit firms should not be thought of in a monopsonistic context has not been subjected to empirical test. So, it appeared desirable to repeat the above adjustment processes, treating all of the types of excluded employers—railroad, government, and non-profit—simultaneously. Specifically, the estimated 1948 employment in each of the following industry groups was computed (the types of large "firms" that might be included within the categories are indicated in parentheses):

Railroads and railway express service (railroads)
Medical and other health services (hospitals)
Educational services, private (private educational institutions)
Educational services, government (public educational institutions)
Public administration ("government")

TABLE 2

AVERAGE[a] PERCENTAGE DIFFERENTIALS[b] FOR TWO SAMPLES OF
AREAS WITH CONCENTRATION RATIOS ADJUSTED FOR THE
PRESENCE OF LARGE RAILROAD, GOVERNMENT,
AND NON-PROFIT FIRMS

Measure	32 Area General Random Sample	25 Area Sample of High Concentration Areas
Overall- 1	51.82	0.00
Overall- 4	74.72	11.18
Overall-10	75.48	18.47
Maximum- 1	51.71	0.00
Maximum- 4	74.73	11.19
Maximum-10	75.50	18.48

[a] All table data are simple arithmetic means.
[b] These differentials were computed by dividing the difference between the adjusted ratios and the unadjusted ratios by the unadjusted ratios.

All employed workers in each of these census categories were considered to be employees of a single firm; the ten largest firms were re-ranked within each area with these five additional "firms" as contenders for any of the top-ranking positions. In nearly all areas three or four of these "firms" actually earned a position among the top ten; concentration ratios were recomputed and average differentials for both samples were determined. The resulting data are reproduced in Table 2.

The general pattern of the data in this table is very much like that found for railroad firms alone: the adjustment process adds successively more to the concentration ratios of one-, four-, and ten-firm data; for any given set of firm data (four-firm data, for example) the adjustment adds proportionately less to concentration ratios as the level of concentration rises; none of these "firms" displaced the largest firm in the twenty-five high concentration areas.

Although the patterns of the averages of the differentials were highly comparable in the two adjustments, their magnitudes were quite different. For example, adjusting the ten-firm concentration ratios for the exclusion of railroads alone brought about an average increase of less than 13 per cent in the thirty-two area general random sample, whereas the same adjustment for railroads, government, and non-profit firms together brought about a 75 per cent increase.

Thus the adjustment for the exclusion of government and non-profit "firms"—though surely overstated in these sample computations—is shown to be the most significant possible source of error in the basic data of this study. The rise in concentration that would take place, if complete and accurate adjustment for these exclusions could be made, might be large. The major conclusion to be drawn from this investigation is that accurate determination of the absolute level of concentration will be impossible until tests of hypotheses concerning the role of government and non-profit firms in monopsonistic activity have been performed and until firm-size distributions are available for railroads, governments, and non-profit firms by labor market area.[21]

6. SUMMARY OF ADJUSTMENTS

The changes brought about by the adjustments described in the preceding sections of this chapter have been expressed in terms of percentages of the unadjusted concentration ratios. These percentages were computed for the individual areas of the various samples used and the results of the operations summarized by means of sample averages. The purpose of this section is that of trying to state in some meaningful fashion the significance of the adjustments for the accuracy of the basic data—which data are to be presented and analyzed in the following chapter. It is assumed that no further warnings need be sounded as to the roughness of the adjustment procedures underlying these summary averages.

The aim of the study is to measure the degree of concentration in the markets for the not-skilled portion of the labor force. Certainly one of the most serious shortcomings of the data lay in the fact that skill breakdowns of workers on a firm basis were not available. So it was necessary to compute concentration ratios using the total employment of large firms as numerators and the total employment of the labor market areas as denominators; these are called Overall concentration ratios. In Section 1 it was concluded that these ratios tend to understate the degree of concentration in not-skilled labor markets by about 16 per cent. Therefore, another set of ratios was constructed which used the same numerators as the Overall ratios but which stripped the skilled, managerial, and professional groups—as well as certain unskilled farm workers—out of the denominators. These ratios are

---

21. Section 12 of the Appendix consists of several miscellaneous elaborations of the data and procedures that have been presented in this section.

called Maximum ratios, and it was estimated in Section 1 that they tend to be about 77 per cent larger than Overall ratios. Thus as far as the problem of the skill composition of the labor force is concerned, it seems reasonably certain that the "true" concentration ratios have numerical values that lie between the Overall and Maximum values, closer to the former than to the latter. The adjustment problems remaining after this bracketing process had been accomplished were concerned with the conceptual and mechanical correctness of these two sets of ratios.

Also examined in Section 1 was the possible error associated with the deletion of the not-skilled agricultural workers from the Maximum denominators. First, nation-wide aggregate data were used to provide an extremely crude estimate: it was that this deletion tends, on the average, to make Maximum concentration ratios about 7 per cent higher than they otherwise would be. Next, the Maximum ratios of individual high concentration areas were adjusted; the results showed the unadjusted ratios of these areas to contain an average overstatement of concentration of about 11 per cent.

In Section 2 an attempt was made to determine the amount of overstatement of concentration in the basic data due to the presence of transitory elements. An appropriate safe guess as to the degree of overstatement resulting from these seasonal and non-seasonal factors appears to be 9 per cent (6 non-seasonal, 3 seasonal) for most areas and 14 per cent (10 non-seasonal, 4 seasonal) for high concentration areas.

In Section 3 the problem of more than one establishment of the same firm being located in the same labor market area was investigated on a sample basis; the errors found were quite small, so that 5 per cent was considered ample allowance for the understatement of the real-world concentration level by the data of this study.

In Section 5 estimates were made of the degree of understatement in the basic data resulting from the exclusion of certain firms from OASI coverage. The adjustment process was broken into two steps because of conceptual uncertainties relating to some of the exclusions. Thus, in the first adjustment procedure, railroads—about which there were no conceptual difficulties—were put into the concentration ratio numerators of two samples; this caused the ratios of the largest, four largest, and ten largest firms of randomly

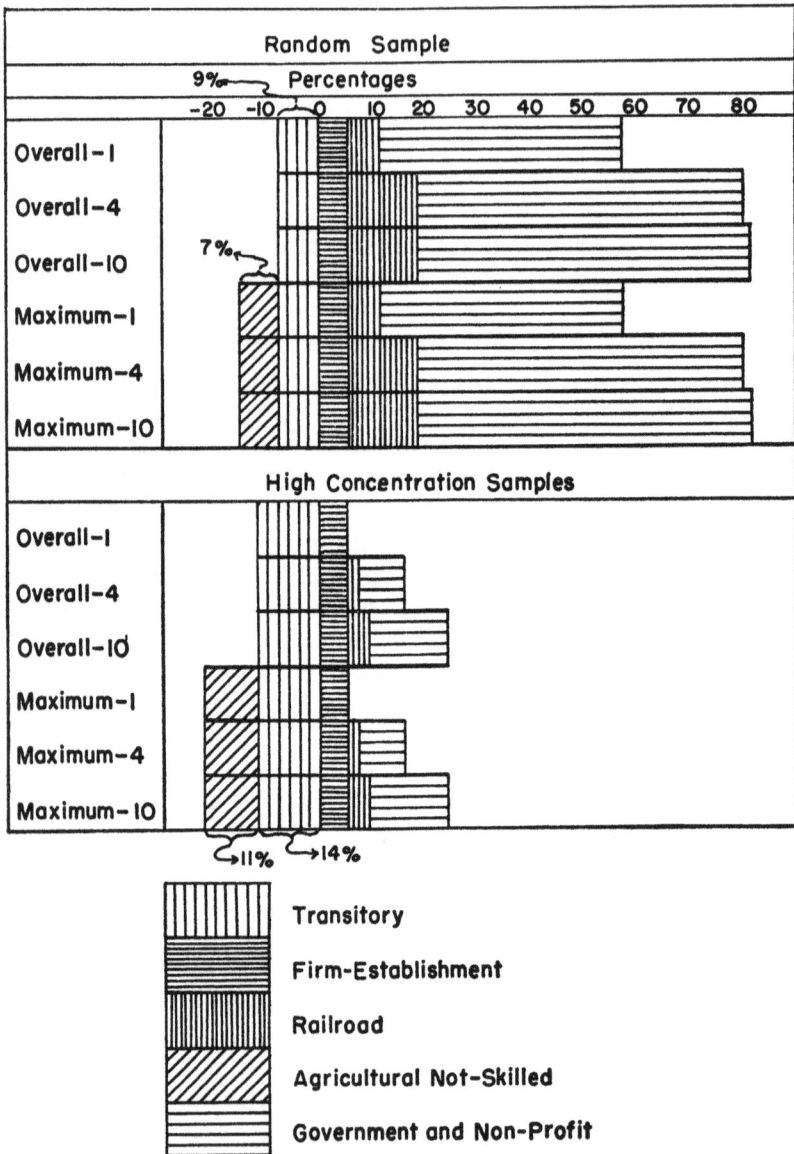

FIG. 2. Bands of Error Resulting from All Adjustments to the
Concentration Ratios of Sample Areas

chosen areas to rise by average amounts of 6, 13, and 13 per
cent respectively and those of high concentration areas to rise
average amounts of 0, 2, and 4 per cent respectively. The
exclusions about which uncertainty was felt were government

and non-profit firms. So an alternative adjustment was performed in which the numerators of sample ratios were adjusted for these types of firms in addition to railroad firms. The resulting increases in concentration were quite large. The average percentage increases brought about in the concentration ratios of the one, four, and ten largest firms were 52, 75, and 75 respectively, for the random sample, and 0, 11, 18 for those of the high concentration sample.

How accurate are these estimates of error? Generalizing on the basis of sample information is unsatisfactory for certain of the problems discussed above, in the sense that there might be—in fact, almost surely are—particular areas for which the actual error may be strikingly larger than that indicated by sample averages. Nevertheless, it is reasonably probable that the adjustments, as averages, err in a properly conservative fashion. The firm-establishment, railroad, and government and non-profit adjustments are too large—grossly so, perhaps, in the case of government and non-profit firms; and, both the agricultural and transitory estimates are probably larger negative numbers than they should be.[22]

The most scientifically precise statement that can be made with assurance is that the correct aggregate degree of error in the basic data probably lies within the limits indicated in Figure 2. This obviously is not a strong statement; its weakness derives primarily from the uncertainties surrounding the desirabilities of the individual adjustments. Until empirical tests have been conducted that provide reliable bases for accepting or rejecting these adjustments, algebraic sums of the above estimates may be misleading.[23]

However, the results can be sharpened considerably by recognizing that the degree of uncertainty about the appropriateness of the various adjustment procedures varies. The desirability of the railroad adjustment is beyond question, strong cases can be made for the firm-establishment and transitory adjustments, and the agricultural not-skilled adjustment would receive support from many economists; the government-and-non-profit-firms adjustment is probably the

22. It should be recalled that the transitory percentage differential is based upon a time interval of one year; if future experimentation should prove this too short, the transitory differentials may become larger negative numbers.

23. The issue under discussion here has to do with the inherent correctness of making the various adjustments—should they, or should they not, be made? This is *not* an expression of concern over the accuracy of the particular estimates that have been arrived at in this chapter.

TABLE 3

AVERAGE PERCENTAGE CHANGES IN BASIC CONCENTRATION DATA
RESULTING FROM ADJUSTMENTS[a]

Measure	Transitory	Firm-Establishment	Railroad	Algebraic Sum: Columns (2), (3), & (4)	Agricultural Not-Skilled[b]	Algebraic Sum: Columns (5) & (6)	Government & Non-Profit	Alebgraic Sum: Columns (7) & (8)
(1)	(2)	(3)	(4)	(5)	(6)	(7)	(8)	(9)
Random Sample Data								
Overall- 1	− 9	5	6	2	0	2	46	48
Overall- 4	− 9	5	13	9	0	9	62	71
Overall-10	− 9	5	13	9	0	9	63	72
Maximum- 1	− 9	5	6	2	− 7	− 5	46	41
Maximum- 4	− 9	5	13	9	− 7	2	62	64
Maximum-10	− 9	5	13	9	− 7	2	63	65
High Concentration Areas Data[c]								
Overall- 1	−14	5	0	−9	0	− 9	0	− 9
Overall- 4	−14	5	2	−7	0	− 7	9	2
Overall-10	−14	5	4	−5	0	− 5	15	10
Maximum- 1	−14	5	0	−9	−11	−20	0	−20
Maximum- 4	−14	5	2	−7	−11	−18	9	− 9
Maximum-10	−14	5	4	−5	−11	−16	15	− 1

[a] See text for descriptions of samples and many qualifications associated with the estimates.
[b] The high concentration estimate (−11) was made on a sample basis; the 7 per cent figure was obtained from aggregate data, not from adjustment of the random sample. See Section 1, this chapter.
[c] Two separate samples were used for these estimates. See text, Sections 1 and 2, this chapter.

only one about which the levels of uncertainty and disagreement would be high. Thus more exact results are obtainable, at little cost in assurance of accuracy, by recognizing these various degrees of certainty in the process of summation. This has been done in Table 3. Column 5 is an algebraic sum of estimates of error for which there is a strong presumption in favor of incorporation into the basic data: these are the errors associated with the railroad, transitory, and firm-establishment problems. The totals suggest that the concentration ratios of the randomly chosen areas should be increased slightly and those of the high concentration areas should be decreased slightly—less than 10 per cent in each case. In the next two columns the agricultural not-skilled adjustment is incorporated into the total error: the effect is to lower the Maximum concentration ratios of the two groups of areas by amounts of 7 and 11 per cent. If, finally, the government-and-non-profit-firms adjustment is included, the random sample aggregate error rises sharply—up to plus 72 per cent for ten-firm data—and the effects upon the high concentration areas are much less pronounced, so that the aggregate sums of these vary from minus 20 per cent for the Maximum-1 ratios to plus 10 per cent for the Overall-10 ratios.

The above statements are generally oriented toward the effects of the adjustments upon the absolute level of concentration. It is necessary to supplement these with a brief comment about the impact of the adjustments upon the rankings of areas. For the agricultural not-skilled, the transitory, and the firm-establishment adjustments, rank correlation coefficients between rankings "before" and "after" were computed; in all cases the coefficients were positive and large. It seems improbable, therefore, that the analysis in Chapter III is jeopardized by the use of unadjusted concentration ratios for ordering purposes. Nevertheless, it may be taken as a certainty that their use does involve serious rank mislocation for some areas—those containing large firms not covered by OASI.[24]

In brief summary, it seems that adjustment of the basic data for the most likely sources of error would show increases and decreases in concentration ratios that would, broadly speaking, tend to offset each other—although "perfect" adjustment for these errors might involve a minor increase in the ratios of most of the areas and a slightly larger decrease in those of high concentration. A certain effect would be to change the rank positions of a few areas upward—perhaps drastically in some cases—because of the presence of railroads or multi-establishment firms. Finally, if future research should reveal that government and/or non-profit firms cannot be distinguished from private profit-seeking firms as regards participation in monopsonistic activity, the crude adjustment procedure used here suggests that much more refined analysis must be accomplished before either the absolute level or ranking indications of the unadjusted concentration ratios of this study can be accepted.

24. Section 13 of the Appendix contains further information about the possibilities of error involved in using unadjusted concentration ratios for ranking purposes.

CHAPTER III

THE EXTENT AND CHARACTERISTICS OF
EMPLOYER CONCENTRATION IN LABOR
MARKETS IN THE UNITED STATES,
MARCH, 1948

1. INTRODUCTION

The purpose of this chapter is that of presenting summaries and analyses of the basic concentration data. The first task, performed in the next section, is that of providing information about the absolute level of concentration prevailing in local labor markets. This is done by presenting cumulative relative frequency distributions of the numbers of areas and employed workers by concentration. Several measures of concentration are used, so the next section is devoted to analyzing the extent to which rankings of areas according to the various measures are in agreement. Although rank correlations of samples of areas show that the extent of agreement is generally quite high, it is considerably less than perfect among high concentration areas; so the individual measures are combined into a single index and this "summary" index is used for the purpose of choosing the 100 most concentrated areas. In Section 4 these 100 areas and all 1,774 areas are separately examined for the purpose of analyzing the variations in size relationships that take place among the ten largest firms as concentration changes; the purpose of this portion of the study is that of finding the extent to which concentration is a single-large-firm phenomenon—as opposed to a phenomenon involving several large firms. The following three Sections (5, 6, and 7) represent attempts to find systematic relationships between concentration and (successively) population size, industry, and region; both the 100 top areas and all 1,774 areas are used in these investigations. Section 8 consists of a brief summary reminder of the aims of the chapter.

2. The Absolute Level of Concentration

The most important contribution that the data of this study may make is that of providing partial answers to questions concerning the general level of concentration prevailing in local labor markets of the United States—questions such as these: How many of the areas studied are "very high" in concentration? What proportion of the labor force is employed in "high" concentration areas?

It will be seen that the answers are not wholly unambiguous. In part the ambiguity concerning the level of concentration grows out of the fact that two sets of concentration ratios were used in an attempt to bracket the "real-world" ratios. The Overall ratios—which have total firm employment as numerators and total area employed labor force as denominators—tend to understate slightly the level of concentration; the Maximum ratios—which have the same numerators as the Overall ratios but which have only the not-skilled employed workers in the denominators—tend to be almost twice as large, on the average, as their Overall counterparts, and thus tend to overstate substantially the level of concentration.

The fact that there is ambiguity concerning the "true" level of concentration within an area—in the sense that the Overall and Maximum data for the area prescribe fairly wide limits within which it may lie—does not necessarily mean that only ambiguous conclusions can be drawn from the data. Table 4 presents cumulative relative frequency distributions of the 1,774 labor market areas according to six concentration measures. There is no uncertainty about the fact that the areas are heavily distributed toward the low-concentration classes. The distribution of areas according to the Overall-1 measure of concentration, for example, shows the largest employer to hire less than 50 per cent of the total employed labor force in 99.7 per cent of the areas studied; i.e., in only three-tenths of 1 per cent of all 1,774 areas—six areas, to be exact—did the largest employer hire as many as 50 per cent of all of the employed workers, according to this measure of concentration. The percentages of areas having concentration ratios of less than 50 per cent according to Overall-4 and Overall-10 were 98.9 and 97.8 respectively. The Maximum estimates, of course, present a picture of somewhat greater concentration. Nevertheless, the percentages of labor market

TABLE 4

CUMULATIVE RELATIVE FREQUENCY DISTRIBUTIONS OF 1,774 LABOR
MARKET AREAS ACCORDING TO SIX MEASURES OF
EMPLOYMENT CONCENTRATION

Concentration Ratio Class	Percentage of Areas in Concentration Ratio Class According to Six Different Measures of Concentration					
(1)	Overall-1 (2)	Maximum-1 (3)	Overall-4 (4)	Maximum-4 (5)	Overall-10 (6)	Maximum-10 (7)
Under 10%	80.5	47.7	46.3	9.9	25.8	1.0
Under 20%	94.6	80.3	82.1	41.7	67.8	19.7
Under 30%	98.4	90.9	93.1	68.5	86.8	45.0
Under 40%	99.5	95.7	97.4	83.4	94.8	67.1
Under 50%	99.7	97.7	98.9	91.3	97.8	81.3
Under 60%	99.8	99.0	99.4	95.4	99.3	89.7
Under 70%	100.0	99.3	99.7	97.8	99.4	94.9
Under 80%		99.5	100.0	98.4	99.9	97.6
Under 90%		99.5		98.9	100.0	98.4
Under 100%		99.7		99.2		98.9
Under 110%		99.7		99.5		99.1
Under 120%		99.8		99.5		99.4
Under 130%		99.9		99.7		99.7
Under 140%		100.0		99.8		99.7
Under 150%				99.9		99.8
Under 160%				100.0		99.9
Under 170%						100.0

areas having concentration ratios of less than 50 per cent according to these three measures are impressively large: 97.7 (Maximum-1), 91.3 (Maximum-4), and 81.3 (Maximum-10).

The fact that the Overall estimates tend to understate concentration means that the figures presented at each concentration level in the Overall distributions of Table 4 are too large; for example, the number of areas which have "true" concentration ratios of less than 50 per cent is probably less than the 99.7 per cent provided by the distribution of areas according to the Overall-1 estimates. On the other hand, the fact that the Maximum estimates tend to seriously overstate concentration means that the figures presented at each concentration level in the Maximum distributions of Table 4 are too small; for example, the number of areas which have "true" concentration ratios of less than 50 per cent is probably greater than the 97.7 per cent provided by the distribution of areas according to the Maximum-1 estimates. Thus these two estimates of the number of areas in which the concentration ratio is less than 50 per cent probably constitute the limits within which the number of areas having "true" concentration ratios of less than 50 per cent lie. Hence, with reference to these particular estimates, it is probably correct to say that the percentage of labor market areas having "true" largest-firm concentration ratios of less than 50 per cent is not less than 97.7 nor greater than 99.7. Moving across the same row of data in Table 4 permits these similar statements: The percentage of areas studied in which the "true" concentration ratio for the four largest firms is less than 50 per cent is not less than 91.3 nor greater than 98.9. The percentage of areas studied having "true" ten-largest-firm concentration ratios of less than 50 per cent is between 81.3 and 97.8.

In order to obtain information concerning the level of employment concentration indicated by ratios involving a much larger number of firms, concentration ratios for the thirty largest firms in each area were computed as follows: the employment of the tenth-largest firm was multiplied by twenty and the product was added to the sum of the employment of the ten largest firms; this was divided by the total employed labor force estimate to obtain "Overall-30" and by the not-skilled labor force estimate to obtain "Maximum-30." Obviously this procedure provides an overstatement of the "true" numerators and hence ratios that are too large.[1] These data are not provided in Table 4, but distributions identical to those of Table 4 were prepared and they show 89.6 per cent of the areas to have concentration ratios of less than 50 per cent according to Overall-30 and 43.0 per cent of the areas to have Maximum-30 ratios of less than 50 per cent.

Finally, it should be noted that concentration ratios considerably in excess of 100 per cent are evident in all of the distributions of areas according to Maximum measures— whereas there are none in the Overall distributions. This provides support for the evidence given in Chapter II indicating that Maximum concentration ratios are biased toward overstatement.

It is clear from Table 4 that the results obtained in measuring the level of concentration in the six different ways represented by the six different types of ratios are all con-

1. The employment of the tenth-largest firm of each area is presented in the master table referred to in footnote 3 of Chapter I. Thus the concentration ratio for any number of firms greater than ten can be estimated in the way described above.

TABLE 5

EMPLOYMENT IN 1,774 LABOR MARKET AREAS ACCORDING TO SIX
MEASURES OF EMPLOYMENT CONCENTRATION

Concentration Ratio Class	Percentage of Employees Employed in Labor Market Areas in Concentration Ratio Class					
	Overall-1	Maxi-mum-1	Overall-4	Maxi-mum-4	Overall-10	Maxi-mum-10
(1)	(2)	(3)	(4)	(5)	(6)	(7)
Under 10%	89.2	74.7	66.8	43.0	46.7	11.1
Under 20%	97.5	91.6	89.9	71.0	79.5	52.1
Under 30%	99.5	96.5	96.0	85.7	91.6	71.2
Under 40%	99.9	98.5	98.8	92.0	96.7	82.8
Under 50%	99.9	99.4	99.7	96.3	99.1	90.4
Under 60%	100.0	99.7	99.8	98.3	99.8	95.3
Under 70%		99.9	99.9	99.4	99.8	97.8
Under 80%		99.9	100.0	99.6	99.9	99.3
Under 90%		99.9		99.8	100.0	99.5
Under 100%		99.9		99.8		99.7
Under 110%		99.9		99.9		99.8
Under 120%		100.0		99.9		99.9
Under 130%				99.9		99.9
Under 140%				99.9		99.9
Under 150%				100.0		99.9
Under 160%						99.9
Under 170%						100.0

sistent with the conclusion that employer concentration is
"high" in only a few labor market areas. It is conceivable,
however, that the few areas that have relatively large concentration ratios are areas which contain disproportionately
large numbers of workers. This possibility is investigated
in Table 5—a table that is very much like Table 4 except that
each area is counted not once but as many times as there are
employees within it.

The data in Table 5 show that employment concentration
is *less* serious when measured by the percentage of employees
in high concentration areas than when measured simply in
terms of the percentage of areas that have high concentration
ratios. Thus all of the percentages of the "Under 50%" row
of Table 5 are larger than the corresponding percentages of
Table 4: that is, according to all six types of concentration
measures, the percentage of the employed labor force working
in areas that have concentration ratios of less than 50 per
cent is greater than the percentage of labor market areas in
this concentration ratio class. Using the upper-and-lower-
limits approach, the concentration circumstances of the 1,774
areas as measured by the four-firm ratios may partially be

described in this manner: the percentage of workers who are employed in labor market areas, the four largest firms of which employ less than 50 per cent of the total labor force, is not less than 96.3 nor greater than 99.7. The corresponding limits for the thirty-firm concentration ratios described above are 65.8 per cent and 92.1 per cent.

The tone of the preceding discussion indicates a belief that the level of concentration, as shown by the data of Tables 4 and 5, is not high.[2] It must be clear, however, that such a conclusion can only be stated with conviction when a great deal more empirical work has been done—when the concentration-monopsony relationship has been more firmly established and when tests have been performed that demonstrate what the crucial levels of concentration are.

3. RANKING LABOR MARKET AREAS BY CONCENTRATION

In the two tables of the preceding section and in the text discussing them each of the six indexes is treated as if it were independent of the others. This is clearly not the case. In each area the six indexes consist of two sets of estimates of

2. A major basis for this belief is provided by an experiment which merits detailed description. This question was raised: Given the 1948 size-distributions of firms and labor markets, to what extent is it possible to raise concentration by relocating firms among labor markets in such a way as to make the concentration ratios in each as large as possible? An unequivocal answer was obtained: the level of concentration could be increased by a very great deal indeed.

The experiment was conducted as follows: Detailed distributions of labor market areas, by size of employed labor force (the Overall denominators), and firms, by employment size, were prepared. Then firms were reallocated among labor market areas with a view toward constructing as many Overall-4 ratios of 50 per cent or more as possible. For example, there were 57 labor market areas with employed labor forces in the 14,000-14,999 size class; all of these were "converted" into "50 per cent or more" areas according to Overall-4 concentration ratios by "placing" in each 1 firm in the 5,000-5,999 employment-size class, 2 firms in the 1,000-1,999 employment-size class, and 1 firm in the 500-999 employment-size class; this obviously conservative procedure "used-up" 57 of a total of 71 firms in the 5,000-5,999 class of the distribution of firms by employment size, 114 of the 2,407 firms in the 1,000-1,999 firm-size class, and so on.

As a result of reallocating firms among labor market areas in the fashion described above, 83.8 per cent of the labor market areas were made into areas with Overall-4 concentration ratios of 50 per cent or more; this compares with the actual percentage of areas in that concentration class of 1.1, as shown in Table 4. Similarly, according to Table 5, 0.3 per cent of the employed labor force in the areas studied here were actually in labor markets having Overall-4 concentration ratios of 50 per cent or more; after the hypothetical reallocation of firms among labor market areas, that percentage had increased to 28.2.

Thus it is clear, from this purely mechanical point of view, that the opportunities for achieving positions of high concentration remained relatively unexploited in U.S. labor markets in 1948.

three different points on the single "true" concentration curve for the area. Within each set the indexes are related in that they are ratios the denominators of which are identical and the numerators of which are successively larger summations of the employment of firms arrayed by employment size: for example, the numerator of Overall-10 consists of the sum of the employment of the ten largest firms and thus includes the numerators of both Overall-1 and Overall-4. As between sets, the indexes may be viewed as three pairs of ratios, each pair of which (e.g., Overall-1 and Maximum-1) have identical numerators but different denominators.

In an elegant presentation of the numbers on which Tables 4 and 5 are based, the three Overall (or Maximum) numbers for each area would have been combined into a single summary number according to some formula

(A) $C = f(x_1, x_4, x_{10})$

where x_1, x_4, and x_{10} are the concentration ratios corresponding to the largest firm, four largest firms, and ten largest firms respectively and C is the single summary number indexing concentration in the area. The best formula would, in the context of this paper, be that combination of the three concentration ratios that best predicted monopsonistic behavior.

The best formula is not known. It seems reasonable to suppose, however, that it has the property:

(B) An increase in any of the concentration ratios, x_1, x_4, x_{10}, the others not decreasing, will increase C, the index of concentration relevant to monopsony in the area.

It follows from this property that the ranking of the 1,774 areas according to any one of the concentration ratios, x_1, x_4, x_{10}, will be the same as the ranking of the areas by the unknown C if there is perfect *rank* correlation among the x's. Rank correlations of less than +1.00 among the x's show conflicting indications among them as to the relative concentration position of at least some of the areas; the further away from +1.00 the actual coefficients are, the more obscure becomes the "true" ranking of areas by concentration and the less certain it is that the particular concentration indications of any one of the measures approximates those concentration indications which would be provided by the "best" summary index.

TABLE 6

RANK CORRELATION AMONG THE CONCENTRATION RATIOS
IN A RANDOM SAMPLE OF 105 AREAS

Among Overall Ratios	Among Maximum Ratios[a]	Between Overall and Maximum Ratios
0-1 with 0- 4: +0.96	M-1 with M- 4: +0.95	0- 1 with M- 1: +0.96
0-1 with 0-10: +0.91	M-1 with M-10: +0.91	0- 4 with M- 4: +0.95
0-4 with 0-10: +0.99	M-4 with M-10: +0.98	0-10 with M-10: +0.95

[a] The rank correlation coefficient between M-4 and M-30 was also computed: it was +0.91.

In order to obtain some notion as to the extent of agreement among rankings of labor market areas by the six concentration measures, rank correlation coefficients were computed for a random sample of 105 areas;[3] the results are presented in Table 6. The ranking of areas according to Overall-4 ratios is very similar to that of Overall-1 ratios; the ranking according to Overall-10 ratios is even more similar to that of Overall-4 ratios; the relationship between the Overall-1 ranking and that of Overall-10 is less strong, but, at +.91, is still extremely high. The fact that this same pattern of relationships exists among the rankings of the sample areas according to the three types of Maximum concentration ratios is, of course, not surprising. The Maximum ratios of each area have the same numerators as Overall ratios and denominators which, though different from Overall denominators, are the same for all three Maximum concentration ratios. The cross-relationships between Maximum and Overall indexes are consistently high. The consistency is to be expected, "built-in" again; the highness of the relationships means that the deletion of "skilled" groups from the denominators of Overall ratios (to produce Maximum ratios) is not seriously disruptive of rank orders—i.e., the "skilled" groups constitute a fairly uniform proportion of the employed labor forces of labor market areas.[4]

3. This sample is described in Section 10 of the Appendix.

4. The disagreement that exists in the rank relationships across the sets of concentration ratios—between Overall-4 and Maximum-4, for example—appears to hinge primarily upon the fact that agricultural workers constitute a larger proportion of the employed labor force in some areas than in others. (It is to be remembered that agricultural workers are a component of the deleted "skilled" group; they are the reason for the quotation marks around the word "skilled.") The areas in which this component of the employed labor force is relatively large rise in Maximum rankings, as compared with their positions in Overall rankings; and an opposite comparative change in rank position occurs among the areas the

Two closely-related observations seem warranted at this point. One, the extent of agreement between the rankings according to largest-firm concentration ratios and the rankings according to the measures involving four and ten firms tentatively suggests that the relative concentration position of an area, however measured, is largely determined by the relative size of its largest firm.[5] Two, although there are differences in the rank positions of the areas as established by the various concentration ratios, the dominant fact is that of generally high agreement. Thus, this investigation of the 105 area random sample strongly suggests that rankings according to the "best" summary index would not differ greatly from rankings according to any one of the six sets of concentration ratios.

However, the sample on which Table 6 is based was drawn from the whole group of 1,774 areas, whereas there is somewhat greater interest in the identification and study of the areas of highest concentration. The evidence presented thus far does not make it certain that the final conclusion of the preceding paragraph is applicable to the upper portions of the distributions of labor market areas by concentration. According to property (B) above, an area cannot be ranked high in concentration if it does not rank high according to at least one of the concentration ratios. Therefore, the areas were ranked by each of the six ratios and all areas among the top eighty-nine in one or more of the six rankings were selected for further investigation. (The number eighty-nine was obtained by taking 5 per cent of 1,774; these areas will be referred to as "top 5 per cent" areas.)

If the six different ratios were in perfect agreement in ranking areas of high concentration, the six lists of top 5 per cent areas would be identical and the total number of areas appearing on at least one list would be eighty-nine. If, on the other hand, there were no agreement among the measures—if no area were among the top 5 per cent of two separate lists—the total number of top 5 per cent areas would be 534: 89 times 6. Actually, the total number of areas appearing on at least one of the six lists was 150. The fact that this number is as small as it is constitutes a definite, if imprecise,

---

agricultural component of which is relatively small. (The analysis from which this conclusion was drawn is described in the Appendix, Section 14.)

5. The fact that the measures are not independent was noted earlier and will be given explicit attention in the next section of this chapter.

TABLE 7

LOCATION OF 150 TOP 5 PER CENT AREAS AMONG 1,774 AREAS
RANKED BY SIX CONCENTRATION MEASURES

1,774 Areas Ranked According to	Area Ranked 89		Area Having Smallest Ratio Among 150 Top 5 Per Cent Areas	
	Concentration Ratio	Percentile Rank	Concentration Ratio	Percentile Rank
Overall- 1	20.15	95	7.23	71
Overall- 4	32.72	95	15.11	70
Overall-10	39.61	95	17.34	60
Maximum- 1	36.81	95	14.38	68
Maximum- 4	58.35	95	37.65	81
Maximum-10	69.75	95	48.92	81

indication of agreement among the concentration ratios as to which are the high-ranking areas. These 150 areas, comprising 8.5 per cent of the 1,774 areas, contained 2,256,521 employed workers—4.3 per cent of the employed labor force of the 1,774 labor market areas.

Further information about the extent of agreement among the ratios in selecting areas of high concentration is presented in Table 7. It briefly describes the location of the 150 top 5 per cent areas within each of the six distributions. The figures in the first row of the table, for example, may be interpreted as follows: 89 of the 150 top 5 per cent areas have Overall-1 concentration ratios of 20.15 or above and the lowest-ranking of these eighty-nine areas has a percentile rank of 95; the other 61 areas have Overall-1 concentration ratios smaller than 20.15 but as large or larger than 7.23, and the lowest percentile rank among them is 71. The information about the 61 areas is the important content of the table. By way of emphasizing what it has to contribute to an understanding of the extent of agreement among the measures, it may be restated as follows: No area having a percentile rank of less than 71 in the Overall-1 distribution of areas is among the top 5 per cent areas of any distribution. More generally, the table shows that all top 5 per cent areas are ranked well above the medians of all distributions. Finally, these data seem to point to the Maximum-4 and Maximum-10 rankings of high concentration areas as the ones which are least in conflict with those of the other types of concentration ratios; that is, none of the areas ranked among the top 5 per cent areas by

TABLE 8

NUMBER OF TOTAL (150) TOP 5 PER CENT AREAS APPEARING IN
CERTAIN COMBINATIONS OF LISTS OF 89 TOP 5 PER CENT AREAS

0-1, 0-4	0-1, 0-10	0-4, 0-10	0-1, 0-4, 0-10	M-1, M-4	M-1, M-10	M-4, M-10	M-1, M-4, M-10	0-1, M-1	0-4, M-4	0-10, M-10	All Six
57	49	78	48	57	52	78	49	77	69	67	36

other concentration ratios is below percentile rank 81 in either
the Maximum-4 or the Maximum-10 frequency distribution.

The fact that there are only 150 different areas among the
six lists of top 5 per cent areas indicates that some areas are
common to two or more lists. Table 8 provides more specific information about such areas. It shows, for example,
that the six lists of eighty-nine areas have thirty-six areas
(40 per cent) in common; both the three Overall lists and the
three Maximum lists have more than one-half of their top 5
per cent areas in common. The pattern of areas in common
among the three Overall lists is, as would be expected, much
like that among the Maximum lists. Examining either of
these sets of three lists leads toward the conclusion that the
change that is seen as the largest firm, four largest firm, and
ten largest firm concentration lists are viewed successively is
primarily associated with the change from one to four large
firms in the numerators of concentration ratios. The one-
firm lists have only a few more areas in common with the four-
firm lists than with the ten-firm lists, whereas the four-firm
lists have a great deal more areas in common with the ten-
firm lists than with the one-firm lists. The Overall-Maximum
cross comparisons (O-1, M-1; O-4, M-4; O-10, M-10) all show
large numbers of areas in common; the lowest number is sixty-
seven and that is 75 per cent of the total of eighty-nine.

The data in Table 8 are suggestive of high agreement
among the rankings of top 5 per cent areas, whereas those of
Table 7 definitely indicate that there will be some areas that
will be ranked quite differently by the various concentration
ratios. Table 9 shows both indications, in a sense, to be correct. The Overall-Maximum cross comparisons and the four-
ten comparisons are all reasonably high, but the one-four rank
correlation coefficients are not great and the one-ten coefficients
are only +.32 and +.29. All of these coefficients are smaller

TABLE 9

RANK CORRELATION AMONG THE CONCENTRATION RATIOS
OF 150 TOP 5 PER CENT AREAS

Among Overall Ratios	Among Maximum Ratios	Between Overall and Maximum Ratios
0-1 with 0- 4: +0.53	M-1 with M- 4: +0.56	0- 1 with M- 1: +0.89
0-1 with 0-10: +0.32	M-1 with M-10: +0.29	0- 4 with M- 4: +0.72
0-4 with 0-10: +0.92	M-4 with M-10: +0.87	0-10 with M-10: +0.70

than those (of Table 6) which show rank relationships among the 105 areas randomly drawn from the whole population of 1,774 areas.

Abstracting from the sorts of problems discussed in Chapter II, there can be no doubt that the areas that are highest in concentration among the 1,774 areas are included within the 150 top 5 per cent areas. The evidence presented in the preceding pages, however, shows some disagreement among the six measures as to which of the 150 these are. It would be desirable—for certain operations to be performed in later sections of this chapter—to have a refined list of most concentrated areas consisting of the 150 areas less those which might be classified as "borderline" areas: areas whose high concentration position is most in dispute. For purposes of compiling such a list, some device is needed which arbitrates among the conflicting indications of the six measures. The following formula is such a device and the summary number, C', was computed for all 150 top 5 per cent areas:[6]

(C) $C' = 2x_1 + 4.5x_4 + 3x_{10}$

It was stated earlier that a summary formula having property (B) must rank areas very much like the individual x's if rank correlations among the x's were high. In fact,

6. C' is simply the area under the broken-line concentration curve illustrated in the figure below.

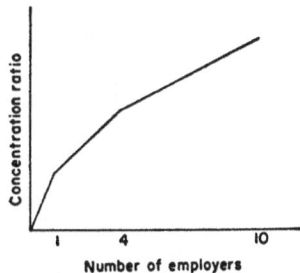

formula (C) above does have property (B) but, as Table 9 shows, certain of the rank correlations among the x's are not particularly high. Thus the acceptance of the formula was tentatively based only on its intuitive satisfactoriness.

C' was calculated for each of the 150 top 5 per cent areas using both Overall and Maximum x's, and for each area the simple mean of Overall and Maximum C' was computed. The 100 areas ranking highest according to this last mean were then considered as the "top 100" areas.

By way of conducting simple checks on the acceptability of the summarizing formula, these brief operations were performed:

1. Of the 150 top 5 per cent areas, 36 were in all 6 lists of 89 areas. It seems reasonable to expect a good summary index to rank these areas relatively high. In fact, all of them were included among the top 100 areas, none ranking below rank 55.

2. Of the top 5 per cent areas, 21 were in only one of the 6 lists of 89 areas. It seems reasonable to expect a good summary index to rank these areas relatively low. In fact, none of the 21 areas was included among the top 100 areas.

3. The 20 areas ranking highest according to the summary index were used for computing rank correlation coefficients. The coefficients express the relationships between the areas as ranked by the summary measure and as ranked by the other 6 measures. They are as follows:

Summary, Overall- 1: +.68   Summary, Maximum- 1: +.59
Summary, Overall- 4: +.67   Summary, Maximum- 4: +.90
Summary, Overall-10: +.59   Summary, Maximum-10: +.79

These investigations would seem to warrant, for purposes of further study, the acceptance of the top 100 as provided by the formula for C'. It is not pretended that this formula is the "best" formula for C in the sense discussed earlier; it is contended only that C' represents a reasonable means of reconciling differences among the six measures, that it will rank the areas in approximately the same order as do the x's, and that the ranking by C' therefore will not seriously misrepresent the facts of the underlying data.

These top 100 areas comprise 5.6 per cent of the 1,774 areas studied and contain 2.6 per cent of the total employed labor force in those 1,774 areas. Table 10 summarizes the concen-

TABLE 10

SELECTED CONCENTRATION RATIOS FOR TOP 100 AREAS RANKED
BY SIX MEASURES OF CONCENTRATION

Rank of Area	Concentration Ratio of Area					
	Overall-1	Overall-4	Overall-10	Maximum-1	Maximum-4	Maximum-10
1	68	75	89	134	153	164
10	36	64	70	79	106	122
20	33	50	55	57	88	105
30	29	45	52	53	77	89
40	27	42	49	48	69	82
50	24	39	47	42	66	77
60	23	37	44	39	63	74
70	20	34	40	34	62	71
80	18	33	38	30	59	70
90	15	30	34	26	56	67
100	10	26	29	17	48	58

tration ratios, the x's, for these areas, by providing the ratios of the highest-ranking area and every tenth-ranking area for 6 separate rankings of these areas. It provides therefore the same sort of information as that of Table 7, in that it describes the location of these 100 areas within the high concentration portions of the 6 arrays of 1,774 areas. In so doing, it underlines the fact, apparent or implicit in certain of the data presented in previous tables, that all of the frequency distributions are skewed heavily "to the right"—toward high concentration. Or, to state it differently, the data emphasize how few high concentration ratios there are by showing how rapidly fairly "low" concentration ratios are encountered in moving "down" rankings of the 100 top areas.

4. THE SHAPE OF THE CONCENTRATION CURVE

The question of the shape of the concentration curve can be raised in this fashion: To what extent is it true that areas ranking high in concentration have high concentration because of the dominance of one or a few (two, three, or four) very large firms rather than the presence of several (say, ten) moderately large firms of approximately equal size? The question thus is one of relative inequality of size among the largest firms in the areas. There was a good deal of evidence on this problem contained in the tables of the preceding section;[7] here the matter will be given more direct attention.

7. For example: rows 1 and 4 of Table 7 show that all areas high in concentration according to four- and ten-firm concentration ratios are located in the top one-third of areas as ranked by one-firm concentration ratios.

TABLE 11
SELECTED INEQUALITY RATIOS FROM TOP 100 AREAS

Concentration Rank of Area According to Summary Index (1)	Median Value[a] of Inequality Ratio[b] in Concentration Rank Class		
	X_1/X_4 (2)	X_1/X_{10} (3)	X_4/X_{10} (4)
1 to 20	.746	.721	.922
21 to 40	.656	.573	.910
41 to 60	.602	.541	.887
61 to 80	.521	.443	.866
81 to 100	.608	.538	.870

[a] The median values shown in this table are for each kind of ratio and each concentration class the tenth highest ratio observed in the class.
[b] The X's of these ratios are firm employment figures; the subscripts indicate the number of firms involved. Thus X_1/X_4 is the ratio of the employment of the largest firm to the sum of the employments of the four largest firms.

For each of the top 100 areas the following three employment ratios were computed:

$$X_1/X_4, \ X_1/X_{10}, \text{ and } X_4/X_{10}.$$

These ratios, of course, are the same for both the Overall and Maximum concentration ratios. The first of the ratios indicates the extent to which the largest firm dominates the four largest firms; the second, the extent of dominance of the largest firm in the ten largest; and the third, the dominance of the four largest firms. Table 11 summarizes these ratios for the top concentration areas, and thereby provides a picture of a striking degree of dominance. Column (2) of that table shows that the largest firm accounts for more than 50 per cent of the employment of the four largest firms of each of the selected five areas. Column (3) shows the dominance of the largest firm to be great even in regard to the ten largest firms, and column (4) draws attention to the fact that the extent of dominance of the four largest firms among the ten largest is very great indeed. Finally, all columns provide clear indications that the extent of dominance declines with the degree of concentration. This view of the top 100 areas suggests that a more detailed investigation of all 1,774 areas might be fruitful.

The Maximum-4 frequency distribution of 1,774 areas was used as a means of dividing the areas into the 10 concentration classes of Table 12, each of which contains either 177 or 178 areas. The data in the first row of Table 12 concern the 177 areas that constitute the highest concentration 10 per cent

TABLE 12

INEQUALITY DATA BASED ON 1,774 AREAS RANKED BY
MAXIMUM-4 CONCENTRATION RATIOS

Areas Ranked[a] (1)	Inequality Ratios Based on Aggregate Employment Data for Concentration Rank Class[b]					
	E_1/E_{1-4} (2)	E_1/E_{1-10} (3)	E_{1-4}/E_{1-10} (4)	E_{2-4}/E_{1-10} (5)	E_{5-10}/E_{1-10} (6)	E_{2-4}/E_{1-N} (7)
1- 177	.569	.482	.846	.364	.154	.156
178- 354	.512	.396	.773	.378	.227	.117
355- 531	.504	.366	.727	.361	.273	.090
532- 709	.462	.318	.688	.371	.312	.083
710- 886	.447	.305	.682	.377	.318	.072
887-1,064	.435	.280	.644	.364	.356	.063
1,065-1,241	.441	.284	.644	.360	.356	.055
1,242-1,419	.395	.235	.595	.360	.405	.047
1,420-1,596	.383	.230	.601	.371	.399	.039
1,597-1,774	.334	.188	.562	.374	.438	.022

[a] These are not unique groupings of areas. See footnote 8, Chapter III.
[b] The letter "E" means "the aggregate employment in the class," and the subscripts indicate the number of firms involved. Thus E_{2-4} means the total employment of all firms ranking second, third, and fourth in all 177 (or 178) areas in the class. The designation E_{1-N} refers to the total employment of all firms in all areas of the class.

of the 1,774 areas in the Maximum-4 frequency distribution, the next row of data concern the 177 areas which are next-highest in concentration, and so on.[8]

Inequality ratios highly comparable to those of Table 11 were prepared for the ten classes of areas by using the sums of the numerators of the concentration ratios within the classes. Thus in the ratio E_1/E_{1-4}, E_1 is the sum of the 177 (or 178) numerators of the Maximum-1 (or Overall-1) concentration ratios—and, therefore, represents the sum of the employment of all of the largest firms in the areas—and E_{1-4} represents the sum of the numerators of the Maximum-4 (or Overall-4) concentration ratios of these areas. Hence, the ratios E_1/E_{1-4}, E_1/E_{1-10}, E_{1-4}/E_{1-10} are exactly the same as the ratios of Table 11 except that these involve a large number of areas in each class whereas those of Table 11 involve only one.

Columns (2), (3), and (4) of Table 12 show the extent of dominance among the high concentration areas to be consistent with the data of Table 11. Thus the largest firm in the high concentration areas hires 56.9 per cent of the workers employed by the four largest firms and 48.2 per cent of those employed by the ten largest firms. The largest firms among

8. The class interval of the Maximum-4 array used for this purpose was one percentage point. Areas were not ranked within these classes, and therefore, the particular groupings of 177 or 178 used in Table 12 are not unique.

these high concentration areas, then, employ more workers than the firms ranking two through four and almost as many as firms ranking two through ten. In these same high concentration areas, the four largest firms together employ 84.6 per cent of the workers hired by the largest ten firms. Moving down these three columns shows the extent of dominance to fall off more or less smoothly as concentration declines. If there were no inequality among the ten large firms of low concentration areas—if all ten employed the same number of workers—the first three ratios in the bottom row of the table would be .250, .100, and .400. In fact, they are .334, .188, and .562. There is mild inequality among the areas of lowest concentration.

Looking only at the information in columns (2) and (4) of Tables 11 and 12, one can infer that, as concentration decreases, the size of the largest firm decreases in relation to that of the ten largest combined and the combined size of firms ranking five through ten increases in relation to the ten largest combined. What is *not* directly clear is the change that takes place in the combined size of firms ranking two, three, and four.

Columns (3), (5), and (6) of Table 12 provide direct information about the changes that take place in the relative sizes of these three groupings of firms: the largest; firms ranking two, three, and four; and firms ranking five through ten. It is interesting to note that the relative combined size of firms two through four stays about constant. This means, then, that firms two through four play, in a sense, a "passive" role in the changes shown in columns (2), (3), and (4). The basic "active" elements shown in the data of these columns are the steady decline in relative position by the largest firm (as concentration decreases) and the compensatory rise in the combined relative size of firms five through ten.

The classes of areas in Table 12 are ranked according to Maximum-4 concentration ratios. Column (7) of that table represents an attempt to determine whether firms two, three, and four are equally "passive" in their influence upon the four-firm concentration ratios—to determine, in other words, whether these firms contribute to the decrease in concentration. Thus column (7) measures the combined size of the second, third, and fourth firms as a proportion of the estimated employment of *all* firms of all areas in the class; the

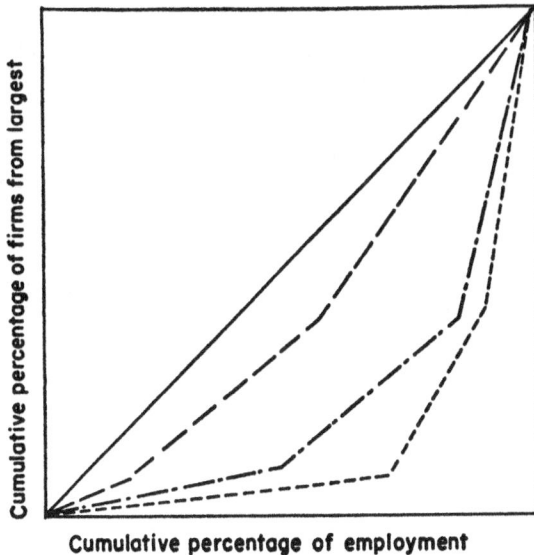

FIG. 3. Lorenz Curves Showing Relative Sizes of Ten Largest Firms
for Three Groups of Areas

steady decrease in this proportion (again, as concentration decreases) indicates that these firms definitely are "positive" determinants of the four-firm concentration positions—that is, the concentration positions of the areas are a partial reflection of the fact that the combined size of the second, third, and fourth firms decreases as a proportion of the total employed labor force.[9]

9. This is implied by the earlier finding (see Table 6) that the rank correlation coefficients between rankings according to one-firm ratios and four-firm ratios are not +1.00. The same coefficients, because they are so large (+.95 and +.96),

The Lorenz curves in Figure 3 might be thought of as abbreviated visual summaries of this investigation: they show that increasing concentration is associated with increasing inequality among the ten largest firms. Perhaps the most striking aspect of this inequality is the fact that, in general, the firms ranking five through ten suffer a severe loss in relative position: among the areas of low concentration these firms together account for 43.8 per cent of the employment of the ten largest firms, whereas in the highest ranking 10 per cent of the areas, that percentage has fallen to 15.4— about 2.5 per cent per firm. It seems clear that high concentration generally is a phenomenon of a few firms at most; within these few firms, the largest firm dominates heavily, tending to have more employees than the next three largest firms combined.

5. Concentration and Community Size

In Section 2 of this chapter it was noted briefly that Tables 4 and 5 suggest a marked tendency for areas high in concentration to have smaller labor forces than areas of low concentration. This matter is explored at greater length in this section.

Return to Tables 4 and 5. Comparison of column (6) of Table 4 with column (6) of Table 5 shows that the areas with Overall-10 ratios of less than 10 per cent comprised approximately 26 per cent of the 1,774 areas but contained approximately 47 per cent of the 1,774 areas' employed workers; thus the lowest concentration areas were almost twice as large, in terms of labor force per area, as the average of the 1,774 areas. On the other hand, the areas with Overall-10 ratios of 50 per cent and above, comprising 2.2 per cent of the areas, contained only 0.9 per cent of the labor force and thus were less than one-half as large, in terms of employed labor force, as the average area.

Tables 4 and 5 are not conveniently arranged for reading the kind of relation between concentration and community size given in the previous paragraph. Therefore, the data were rearranged as follows: the areas were ranked by concentration as in Tables 4 and 5, and five concentration classes set up with each class containing 20 per cent (354 or 355) of

---

imply that the influence of the second, third, and fourth firms in this regard is not great.

TABLE 13

RELATIVE SIZE OF LABOR FORCE PER AREA AND CONCENTRATION

Area Concentration Rank	Ratio of Mean Labor Force Per Area in Concentration Class to Mean Labor Force Per Area in All Classes According to Six Indexes of Concentration					
	Overall-1	Overall-4	Overall-10	Maxi-mum-1	Maxi-mum-4	Maxi-mum-10
1- 354	.592	.562	.635	.430	.480	.515
355- 709	.539	.610	.727	.519	.519	.511
710-1,064	.697	.803	.720	.557	.488	.640
1,065-1,419	1.113	.753	.807	.843	.839	.719
1,420-1,774	2.059	2.272	2.112	2.651	2.674	2.615

the areas. For each such class, total employment was expressed as a ratio to the total employment of all classes. These employment ratios multiplied by five show for each concentration class the ratio of the average size, in terms of employment, of the areas in the class to the average size of all 1,774 areas. These ratios are given in Table 13.

In general, Table 13 shows what the earlier tables suggested would be shown: for all six rankings, the high concentration areas tend to be smaller in employed labor-force size than the low concentration areas; more specifically, the areas of high concentration tend to be about one-half as large and the low concentration areas tend to be more than twice as large as the mean of all 1,774 areas. The data also indicate, however, that this inverse relationship between community size and concentration is not perfect. In all of the rankings except one (Maximum-1) there is one point at which a concentration class has a larger ratio than the class ranking next below it. For example, the top concentration class in the Overall-1 ranking of areas has a ratio of .592 whereas the class below it has a ratio of only .539; the average size of the 354 areas in the first class is greater than that of the 355 areas in the second class.

It should also be noted that the ratios of the Maximum rankings show a steeper progression than do those of the Overall rankings—the inverse correlation is greater in the Maximum ranking. A difference between Maximum and Overall rankings was noted in Section 3 of this chapter. At that time this difference was seen to be primarily an outgrowth of the exclusion of agricultural workers from Maximum denominators. The proportion of these workers varies considerably from county to county and the effect of such variation is to increase the rank position of those areas in which the proportion is large and decrease the rank position of those areas in which it is small. Combining this finding with the observed differences between the Overall and Maximum ratios as shown in Table 13 leads to the conclusion that the less populous areas are those in which the agricultural component is relatively large and vice-versa.

Another way of expressing the same ideas contained in the above paragraph is to say that the Maximum rankings more closely approximate rankings based on concentration ratios computed for the non-agricultural economy than do Overall rankings and that the inverse correlation between community size and concentration is more pronounced in the non-agricultural economy than in the total economy.

In Table 13 concentration is treated, in a sense, as the independent variable and community size as the dependent variable. For purposes of extending the analysis this relationship was reversed. The areas were distributed among ten size classes the limits of which were chosen in such a way as to include roughly 10 per cent of the areas within each class. Each of these ten classes was ranked according to each of the six concentration measures and medians were determined; means for each measure (in each class) were also computed. These data are shown in Table 14.

TABLE 14

SIZE OF LABOR FORCE AND CONCENTRATION

Number of Persons in Labor Force Per Area	Percentage of Areas in Class	Percentage of Labor Force in Class	Over-all-1		Over-all-4		Over-all-10		Maximum-1		Maximum-4		Maximum-10	
			Median	Mean	Median	Mean	Median	Mean	Median	Mean	Median	Mean	Median	Mean
0- 3,999	10.8	1.0	8	10.9	14	17.7	15	21.8	19	24.1	34	38.5	43	47.5
4,000- 5,499	9.9	1.6	5	6.9	9	12.5	13	16.1	11	16.0	20	28.7	32	37.3
5,500- 6,999	11.2	2.4	4	6.4	11	11.7	13	15.4	10	14.3	22	26.2	32	34.5
7,000- 8,499	10.4	2.7	4	5.7	9	11.5	12	15.3	9	12.4	20	24.7	29	33.2
8,500- 9,999	9.1	2.8	4	6.0	9	12.1	13	16.6	10	12.8	22	25.6	31	34.8
10,000-12,499	10.3	3.9	5	6.6	11	13.3	16	18.1	10	13.2	23	26.3	33	35.8
12,500-14,999	8.5	3.9	4	5.4	9	12.1	14	17.3	8	10.2	19	22.8	28	32.7
15,000-19,999	8.9	5.2	5	6.4	11	13.1	16	18.2	9	12.0	23	24.2	31	33.9
20,000-34,999	9.8	8.7	5	6.5	12	14.1	18	19.9	9	13.3	22	24.7	33	34.9
35,000 and over	11.3	67.6	3	5.5	9	11.8	15	17.5	5	9.0	15	19.3	24	28.5

The community size-concentration relationship shown in this table is less striking than that of Table 13. In fact, almost all of the significant variation in means and medians occurs in the largest and smallest size categories, the small areas having distinctly higher concentration and the large areas being characterized by lower concentration. If these were deleted from the table, it would be difficult to determine by observation whether the net community size-concentration relationship were positive or negative.

The thing that comes most immediately to mind—by way of trying to reconcile the apparent differences in the community size-concentration relationship as shown by the above two tables—is that the open-end size category "35,000 and over" in Table 14 may conceal large numbers of workers who sell their services in markets whose concentration ratios are especially low. Investigation of that category proves this to be the case. There are twenty-three areas that had estimated 1948 labor forces of 250,000 or more; these areas contained 20.6 million employed workers—39.6 per cent of the total employed labor force investigated in this study and two million more employed workers than are located in the 70 per cent of all areas that comprise the top seven categories of Table 14. The median concentration ratios for these twenty-three areas were all approximately 50 per cent lower than the medians of the whole "35,000 and over" class: Overall-1, one (as opposed to three for the whole class); Overall-4, four (vs. nine); Overall-10, eight (vs. fifteen); Maximum-1, two (vs. five); Maximum-4, seven (vs. fifteen); and Maximum-10, twelve (vs. twenty-four). It is clear, therefore, that the method of presenting the data in Table 14 is misleading in this sense: the bulk of the employed labor force is found in the relatively few large metropolitan centers which constitute the very "bottom" of the "35,000 and over" class; these population centers generally have concentration ratios which are low; the means and medians of the "35,000 and over" class are, therefore, larger than they would be if the concentration ratios of the areas in this class were weighted by employed labor force. The conclusion obviously is that the inverse correlation between community size and concentration is greater, in terms of numbers of workers, than that indicated by the table data. The facts shown in the rest of the table are not discredited, however, and what they show—or seem to show—is that,

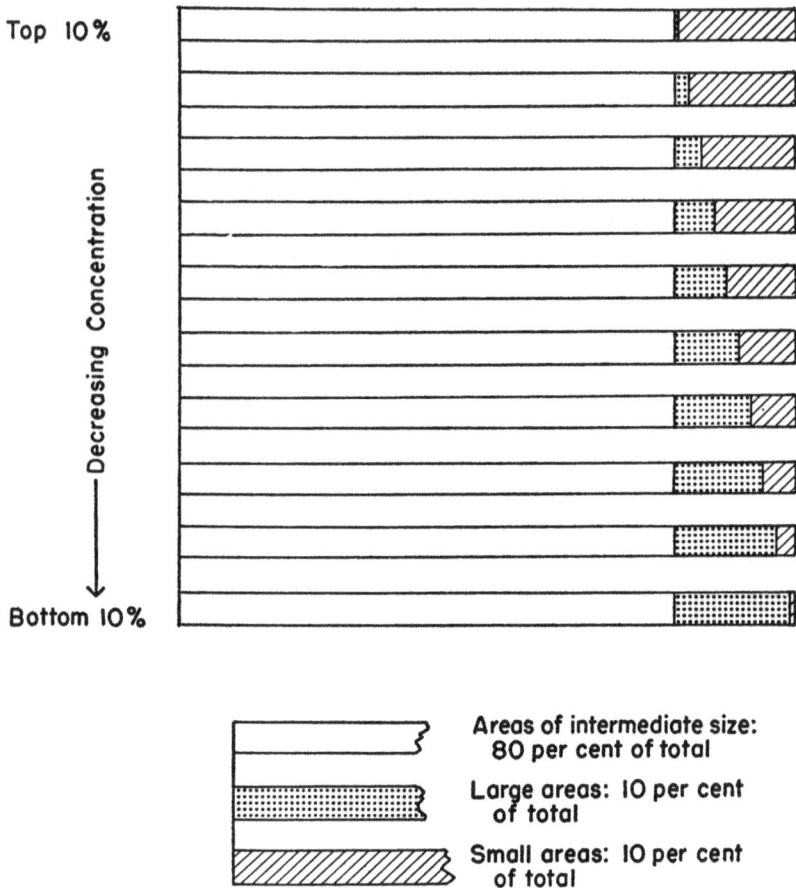

FIG. 4. A Hypothetical Distribution of Three Employment-Size Classes of Labor Market Areas by Concentration

except for the very large and very small areas, the inverse relationship is weak or even, perhaps, non-existent.

The relationship suggested by Tables 13 and 14 is shown in Figure 4. Here the 1,774 areas are ranked by one of the concentration measures and broken into 10 classes—each with an equal number of areas. Within these classes, areas are grouped by employment size: small, intermediate, and large. The intermediate-size group is shown to comprise 80 per cent of the areas and to be distributed uniformly through all concentration classes; the other two groups comprise 10 per cent (each) of the areas and vary in opposite ways in their distribution by concentration. Thus, as concentration decreases, the classes of areas are seen to consist of a constant proportion of intermediate areas, proportionately fewer small areas, and proportionately more large ones.

There are, however, two aspects of this hypothetical interpretation of the relationship between concentration and labor-force size which are not entirely satisfactory. First, if the concentration-labor-force size relationship is strong among the very large and very small areas, one is led to suspect that the relationship runs more pervasively throughout the data; second—and in the same vein—the relationship expressed in Table 13 appears to be so strong as to support the notion that, in fact, the inverse correlation applies to areas of intermediate labor force size also. These considerations dictated some review of the data shown in Tables 13 and 14.

The 1,774 areas were broken into three groups, according to labor force size. Two of these groups were those (of Table 14) within which there appeared to be an inverse relationship between size and concentration, the smallest (0-3,999) and the largest (35,000 and over); the third consisted of all other areas—that 80 per cent of the 1,774 areas having labor force

TABLE 15
CONCENTRATION AND LABOR FORCE SIZE

Rank of Areas	Labor Force Size								
	0-3,999			4,000-34,999			35,000 and Over		
	Ranges of Concentration Ratios	Number of Areas	Mean Labor Force Size (1,000's)	Ranges of Concentration Ratios	Number of Areas	Mean Labor Force Size (1,000's)	Ranges of Concentration Ratios	Number of Areas	Mean Labor Force Size (1,000's)
Areas Ranked by Overall-4 Concentration Ratios									
Top third	19- 71	68	2.4	14- 75	466	13.0	14-46	60	72.5
Middle third	11- 18	64	2.8	7- 13	502	10.4	7-13	71	132.2
Bottom third	0- 10	60	3.2	0- 6	414	12.2	0- 6	69	306.5
Areas Ranked by Maximum-4 Concentration Ratios									
Top third	43-144	60	2.3	29-153	433	11.9	21-82	64	77.7
Middle third	27- 42	64	2.8	17- 28	491	10.8	11-20	67	133.2
Bottom third	0- 26	68	3.3	0- 16	458	12.8	0-10	69	308.5

sizes varying from 4,000 to 34,999. Each of these groups was ranked according to Overall-4 concentration ratios and divided roughly into thirds; arithmetic means of the labor forces of the resulting nine groups were computed and recorded. Then the three basic groups of areas (labor force size classes 0-3,999, 4,000-34,999, and 35,000 and over) were reranked according to Maximum-4 concentration ratios, again roughly divided into thirds, and new labor force means were computed. The results are presented in Table 15.

Both Overall and Maximum data show what the preceding tables suggest would be shown, and they combine to dispose of the questions concerning the size-concentration relationship among the areas of intermediate size. The inverse relationship between size and concentration is smooth and strong in the large and small community size categories; the data of the intermediate size category, on the other hand, show results highly consistent with those of Table 14—the areas within this category which have relatively high concentration ratios definitely not being smaller in size than the other areas in the category. Parenthetically, it should be observed that the tendency (observed in both Tables 13 and 14) for the inverse relationship to be stronger according to Maximum ratios than according to Overall ratios is in evidence in all three community size groups of this table.

These results give strong support to the indication in Table 14 that the inverse relationship between community size and concentration is weak or nonexistent for approximately 80 per cent of the labor market areas with which this study is concerned. How then can the very strong relationship shown in Table 13 be explained? The answer was suggested above: Table 13 expresses the relationship between concentration and employed labor force—or, to put it differently, between concentration and labor market areas as weighted by their employed labor forces. Thus it puts much more emphasis upon the areas located in the bottom, "35,000 and over," category of Table 14; these areas contain *two-thirds* of the total employed labor force and, as shown in the table above, the concentration-labor-force size inverse relationship is very strong among them. It is these areas almost exclusively that explain what is seen in Table 13.

This conclusion is borne out by an experiment the results of which are shown in Table 16. The 1,774 areas were ranked

TABLE 16

PERCENTAGE OF LABOR FORCE AND PERCENTAGE OF AREAS
CONTRIBUTED BY THREE GROUPS OF AREAS,
FOR FIVE CONCENTRATION CLASSES

Concentration Class[a]	Labor Force Size of Areas		
	0-3,999	4,000-34,999	35,000 and Over
Labor Force Percentages			
A (15-75)[b]	2.3	53.6	44.0
B (9-14)	1.8	39.3	58.9
C (5- 8)	1.1	41.1	57.8
D (4)	0.0[c]	11.5	88.5
E (1- 3)	0.0[c]	12.0	88.0
Percentages of Areas			
A (19-75)	19.2	71.5	9.3
B (13-18)	12.7	77.8	9.5
C (9-12)	12.7	74.6	12.7
D (6- 8)	7.5	84.4	8.1
E (1- 5)	2.2	81.4	16.4

[a] Areas ranked from high to low according to Overall-4 concentration ratios. Category "A" contains those top-ranking areas which contain roughly 20 per cent of the total employed labor force. The figures in parentheses show the Overall-4 concentration ratio span of the areas in the category. In the "Percentages of Areas" portion of the table, exactly the same ranking of areas by Overall-4 concentration ratios was used. These categories are different from the ones above them in that they contain roughly 20 per cent of the areas. Thus category "A" contains the 20 per cent of the areas ranking highest in concentration.

[b] Row figures do not add to 100.0; rounding error.

[c] Less than one-half of 1 per cent.

according to Overall-4 concentration ratios; the resulting array was then broken into five categories (A, B, C, D, E) in such a way that each category contained approximately 20 per cent of the total employed labor force. Each of these portions of the labor force was broken down according to the size categories used in the previous table, 0-3,999, 4,000-34,999, and 35,000 and over; that is, the areas of each category (A, B, C, D, E) were divided into three groups according to labor force size and the labor force total of each was expressed as a percentage of the category total. Thus the first row in the table shows that 2.3 per cent of the labor force in category "A" (which contains areas with Overall-4 concentration ratios fifteen through seventy-five) is provided by areas in the small-size class, 53.6 per cent of the labor force in category "A" is provided by areas in the intermediate-size class (4,000-34,999), and 44.0 per cent of the labor force in category "A" is provided by areas in the large-size class.

Examination of the other rows in the table shows that the influence of the large areas is dominant throughout the distribution. The inverse relationship between concentration and labor force size is strong among the small areas also, and to the extent that their weight is felt, they re-enforce the very-large-areas tendency. These data, then, "explain" Table 13.

By way of contrast the bottom portion of the table shows comparable data for areas as they stand without being weighted by labor force size. These areas were also ranked according to Overall-4 concentration ratios. But this time the distribution was broken into five sections, each containing approximately 20 per cent *of the total number of areas,* and each section was analyzed in terms of the percentage of *areas* contributed by the three size groups of areas. Thus the first row in this portion of the table shows that the highest ranking one-fifth of the 1,774 areas consists of small, intermediate, and large areas in the following percentages: 19.2, 71.5, and 9.3. According to this way of viewing the data, the large and small areas exercise about the same aggregate degree of influence upon the concentration characteristics of the distribution; moreover, they are distributed throughout it in such a way that they roughly cancel each other's influence except in the "top" and "bottom" portions. It can be seen that this part of the table does in fact have the general form suggested by Figure 4—except that the intermediate-size areas are shown here to be less "passive" than Figure 4 indicates— and this "explains" Table 14.

Another way of getting at a determination of the relationship between the size and concentration of the labor market areas is by means of rank correlation. The 105-area random sample referred to in Section 3 of this chapter was used for this brief experiment. The areas were ranked by their estimated 1948 employed labor forces and by their Maximum-4 concentration ratios; the correlation coefficient between these two rankings was a weak minus .168. Seen against the background of the preceding explorations, this low coefficient is not surprising.

Table 17 compares the percentage distribution of the 100 top concentration areas among the size categories of labor market areas used in Table 14 with the percentage distribution of all 1,774 areas among these categories. The obvious observations in connection with this table parallel those made

TABLE 17

PERCENTAGE DISTRIBUTIONS OF ALL 1,774 LABOR MARKET AREAS
AND THE 100 TOP CONCENTRATION AREAS AMONG TEN
LABOR FORCE SIZE CATEGORIES

Number of Persons in Labor Force Per Area[a]	Percentage Distributions	
	All 1,774 Areas	The Top 100 Areas
0- 3,999	10.8	25.0
4,000- 5,499	9.9	9.0
5,500- 6,999	11.2	7.0
7,000- 8,499	10.4	7.0
8,500- 9,999	9.1	9.0
10,000-12,499	10.3	10.0
12,500-14,999	8.5	6.0
15,000-19,999	8.9	8.0
20,000-34,999	9.8	10.0
35,000 and over	11.3	9.0
Total	100.2[b]	100.0

[a] Labor market areas are placed in categories on the basis of the 1948 estimates of their labor forces; these same estimates are the denominators of Overall concentration ratios.
[b] Rounding error.

with reference to Table 14. First, the percentages of top concentration areas in all of the size categories except the smallest are about as close to the percentages of all areas in these categories as one would expect to obtain in a random sample of the same size. Second, the smallest-size category, "0-3,999," contains distinctly more top concentration areas than any other class. Finally, the large-area class, "35,000 and over," again conceals a relevant fact: although the percentage of top concentration areas in this category is not out of line, no especially large (in terms of absolute size) areas are included; the largest of the 100 top areas has an estimated employed labor force of slightly more than 100,000 workers, so the very large areas in the "bottom" of the "35,000 and over" category of all 1,774 areas are not represented among the 100 areas of highest concentration.

These 100 areas were also ranked by labor force size and Maximum-4 concentration ratios; the rank correlation coefficient between these two rankings was minus .341.

These results suggest that the inverse correlation among the top 100 areas is more apparent than among all 1,774 areas. This conclusion is supported by two of the three following paragraphs, which describe a more detailed examination of the comparative labor force characteristics of the two groups of areas, as follows:

1. The bottom ("35,000 and over") category of the distribution of all 1,774 areas by labor force size contains 67.6 per cent of the total employed labor force of all 1,774 areas. Whereas the same category contains only 35.3 per cent of the labor force of the 100 top areas. (This is simply a more precise way of restating a point made above: the top 100 areas include none of the extremely large areas.)

2. The top ("0-3,999") category of the distribution of all 1,774 areas by labor force size contains 10.8 per cent of all 1,774 areas and 1.0 per cent of the total employed labor force of the 1,774 areas. This same size category, on the other hand, contains 25.0 per cent of the 100 top areas and 4.2 per cent of the employed labor force of those 100 top areas.

3. The intermediate ("4,000-34,999") category of the 100 top areas contains 66 areas. These were ranked by Overall-4 concentration ratios and divided roughly into thirds. The mean labor forces of these thirds, in thousands, were: top, 11.7; middle, 14.1; and bottom, 11.3. Perhaps the best conclusion these results permit is similar to that for the comparable analysis of the intermediate-size areas in the total distribution: namely, the data definitely do *not* show an inverse correlation between concentration and labor force size.

Thus the analysis of the 100 top areas substantially strengthens the case for there being an inverse relationship between concentration and labor force size. But it also lends support to the notion that this relationship is weak or nonexistent among areas of intermediate labor force size.

Why should there be a tendency for concentration to rise as community size decreases? What sorts of factors could underlie this relationship? A possible answer is that this is purely the result of the random geographical distribution of establishments. To see how this could be, "assume" American local labor market areas and labor force to be distributed geographically exactly as they currently are. Let the areas be ranked by community size. Then suppose that all establishments in the areas are picked up and redistributed among the labor market areas in order of size: large metropolitan areas first, the smaller metropolitan areas next, and so down the community size-ranking of areas. The process by which firms are to be selected for distribution among the areas is to be a random one except for two conditions: first, no establishment can be put into an area "too small" for it, and second, establishments must be distributed so that their aggregate employment opportunities are roughly equal to the number of prospective employees within each area, given the state of economic affairs generally and wage levels particularly.

There will be some labor market areas that are so large relative to present maximum sizes of establishments that no possible distribution of establishments could create a condition of "high" concentration in them. At some point, moving down the size continuum, a community size will be encountered which conceivably could be made concentrated by an especially unlikely distribution of the very largest establishments in the nation. The farther below this point any area is, the larger is the number of firms that could, singly or in combination, bring about a reasonably high level of concentration within it, and the greater the possibility that it will receive an establishment which is extremely large relative to its total labor force.

Such a random distribution of establishments among United States labor markets would produce the following: a level of concentration that is quite low for that part of the labor force which is located in the very large metropolitan areas; a tendency (the extent of which would depend upon the characteristics of the frequency distributions of establishments and labor market areas by size) for both the number of concentrated areas and the general level of concentration to increase as area size decreases; and some number of relatively small areas that would be very high in concentration. In sum, there would be a tendency for concentration and labor market size to be inversely related throughout.

The similarities between a distribution of these hypothetical labor markets by concentration and the real-world distributions according to the six concentration measures of this study are great enough to permit the tentative judgment that this random hypothesis has much to offer by way of explaining the concentration-community-size relationship. The question that immediately arises is: Why does not this inverse relationship show up as strongly in the data as the random hypothesis suggests it should? More specifically: what is the explanation of the lack of a clear-cut relationship among the areas of intermediate size?

One factor that obviously plays a role is agricultural employment. This is shown in several of the preceding tables by the fact that the concentration-community-size relationship is considerably stronger among the Maximum distributions than among the Overall distributions; and the difference between rankings according to these two sets of measures has previously been shown to be related primarily to the proportion of the labor force in agriculture. The basis for this may simply be that agriculture, as a space-demanding industry, tends to be relatively more important in smaller (by population) areas; as an extremely small-firm industry, it has a tendency therefore to offset the inverse relationship between concentration and size.

But, this clearly is not a complete answer to the question concerning the imperfection of the random hypothesis; for, as shown by the data in Tables 13, 14, and 15, the inverse correlation between community size and concentration is considerably less than perfect in the Maximum distributions also.

However, the agricultural factor is helpful beyond explaining the difference between Overall and Maximum rankings; it suggests another influence that may be important, one which may be operative in such a way as to make the community-size-concentration relationship less obvious. That influence is industry. The next section will consist of an examination of its relation to concentration.

6. Concentration and the Industrial Composition of the Labor Force

The relation of concentration to industrial composition of the labor force has three different aspects that are brought out by the following questions:

1. Does the relative distribution of the labor force by industry of employment within a labor market area vary systematically with the extent of concentration in the area?

2. When the employment of the firms that are largest in their areas is distributed by industry, is there any systematic difference between this distribution and the distribution of employment of all firms by industry?

3. Is there any tendency for the industrial composition of the employment of firms that are the largest in their areas to vary with the concentration of the areas?

It is well known that employment in some industries—the extractive industries, for example—is distributed disproportionately toward "small" communities and since, according to the findings of the preceding section, concentration tends to be higher among small communities than among large, it is necessary to examine the relations between industry and concentration with community size "held constant."

In Table 18 the 100 top areas—those that ranked highest on the summary index C′ in Section 3 above—were ranked by concentration into three concentration classes. Concentration class 1 contains the thirty-three areas that ranked highest according to the summary index, class 2 the areas that ranked thirty-four through sixty-seven, and class 3 the areas that ranked sixty-eight and below. The areas were also classified by size of the 1948 estimated employed labor force (the Overall denominators); the class limits of these categories were chosen so as to put thirty-four of the top 100 areas in the smallest labor force class and thirty-three areas in each of the medium and large classes. The total labor force for each of the nine concentration-community-size classes obtained by cross classification was then distributed by industry and the percentage of the class labor force in each industry was computed. Next a 100-area sample was drawn in such a fashion as to insure that its size characteristics were very similar to those of the top 100 areas.[10] These 100 comparative areas were distributed among the same three labor force size categories (with thirty-four, thirty-three, and thirty-three areas in the small, medium, and large classes respectively) and the percentage distribution of the labor force by industry was computed for each of these three classes; these areas were *not* classified by concentration. Then, for each of the nine high concentration groups, the industry percentages were divided by the corresponding percentages of the comparative areas in the same *size* category. It is these quotients, multiplied by 100, that are shown in the top three sections of Table 18; the bottom two sections are compressed versions of the top three.

The table's content may be seen most easily by starting at the bottom, which is a summary comparison of all the 100 top areas and all the 100 areas of the comparative sample.

10. The procedure used to obtain this sample, the industrial composition of its labor force, and its concentration characteristics are described in Section 15 of the Appendix.

TABLE 18

THE RELATIVE DISTRIBUTION BY INDUSTRY OF THE LABOR FORCES
OF THE 100 TOP CONCENTRATION AREAS CLASSIFIED BY
CONCENTRATION AND SIZE OF LABOR FORCE

Size of Area Labor Force[e]	Relative[a] Distribution of Labor Force by Industry[b]									
	Agriculture	Mining	Construction	Manufacturing	Transportation, Communication, and Other Public Utilities	Wholesale and Retail Trade	Finance, Insurance and Real Estate	Business and Personal Services	Professional and Related Services	Other[d]
Among the Areas That Ranked[e] 1-33: Concentration Class 1										
0- 5,499[f]	51	764	87	154	115	103	100	113	103	87
5,500-12,499[g]	37	209	98	240	92	95	100	91	94	85
12,500 and over[h]	62	93	91	183	76	72	62	73	144	57
Among the Areas That Ranked 34-67: Concentration Class 2										
0- 5,499[i]	54	343	78	159	110	107	90	163	105	113
5,500-12,499[j]	51	355	80	182	91	94	93	102	89	88
12,500 and over[k]	78	110	55	222	62	76	59	63	71	58
Among the Areas That Ranked 68-100: Concentration Class 3										
0- 5,499[l]	72	450	78	133	121	106	90	102	95	95
5,500-12,499[m]	58	279	107	172	77	88	93	98	92	110
12,500 and over[n]	56	190	60	198	75	84	76	73	82	55
All Areas by Labor Force Size										
0- 5,499	56	564	83	151	115	105	90	116	102	97
5,500-12,499	48	270	96	201	87	92	100	96	92	95
12,500 and over	66	143	63	205	71	79	69	69	87	56
All Areas										
All sizes	57	187	71	201	75	82	75	78	89	65

a The "relatives" of this table express the relationship between the percentages of workers in 100 high concentration areas with those of workers in a sample of 100 other areas by industry. (See Appendix, Section 15, for a description of the procedure by which the 100 areas of the comparative sample were selected.) For example, the percentage of workers in agriculture among the 15 top concentration areas in Concentration Class 1, size category 0-5,499, was 19.1. The comparable percentage among the 34 areas of the comparative sample which fell into this size category was 37.1. The number "51" in the first row, first column of the table, expresses the relationship between these percentages, as obtained by dividing 19.1 by 37.1, and multiplying this quotient by 100.

b Data on the industrial distribution of the area labor forces were obtained from the *County and City Data Book, 1952.* (See: U.S., Bureau of the Census, *County and City Data Book, 1952: A Supplement to the Statistical Abstract of the United States* [Washington: Government Printing Office, 1953], Table 3.) Thus the above industry relatives refer to the year 1950.

e See note "a," Table 17.

At this level the results are clear: both the mining and manufacturing labor force components are approximately twice as large, proportionately, in the areas of high concentration as in those of the comparative sample. Most of what the rest of the table shows is contained, in less detailed form, in the section of the table next above: "All Areas by Labor Force Size." The main point to be noted is that the disproportionality of mining is extremely great in the smallest of the top 100 areas and it becomes less great in the larger areas. Just the opposite holds for manufacturing: the labor force imbalance in the top 100 areas becomes greater with increases in "size."

Since the two groups of 100 areas have comparable community size characteristics, the presumption is that the observed differences in percentage distribution of labor force by industry are related to the difference in concentration levels; and the establishment of this relationship is the primary contribution of the data in Table 18. Beyond this, the results obtained must be used with caution. The comparative sample was not randomly chosen. None of the very high concentration areas could be included within it and the size characteristics of its areas were chosen to approximate closely those of the 100 top concentration areas. One cannot conclude, therefore, that the quantitative differences in the industrial distribution of the labor force between concentrated and *non-concentrated areas in general* are the same as these differences. The importance of these particular quantitative indications lies in the aid they furnish in interpreting differences between the 100 top areas and all areas in the United States. Thus, Table 19 shows that the percentage of labor force in "mining" of highly concentrated areas is more than three times as large as that of the United States as a whole. The fact that it is less than twice as large as the corresponding percentage in the 100 comparative areas indicates that a con-

---

d Includes persons classified in forestry and fisheries, private households, entertainment and recreation services, public administration, and industry not reported.
    e The 100 top concentration areas were ranked by the summary index.
    f Includes fifteen high concentration areas, thirty-four comparative areas.
    g Includes thirteen high concentration areas, thirty-three comparative areas.
    h Includes five high concentration areas, thirty-three comparative areas.
    i Includes twelve high concentration areas and the same thirty-four comparative areas identified in note "f" above.
    j Includes eight high concentration areas and the same thirty-three comparative areas identified in note "g" above.
    k Includes fourteen high concentration areas and the same thirty-three comparative areas identified in note "h" above.
    l Includes seven high concentration areas and the same thirty-four comparative areas identified in notes "f" and "i" above.
    m Includes twelve high concentration areas and the same thirty-three comparative areas identified in notes "g" and "j" above.
    n Includes fourteen high concentration areas and the same thirty-three comparative areas identified in notes "h" and "k" above.

TABLE 19

PERCENTAGE DISTRIBUTIONS BY INDUSTRY OF THE LABOR FORCES
OF 100 TOP CONCENTRATION AREAS, 100 COMPARATIVE AREAS,
AND ALL AREAS IN THE UNITED STATES

Industry	Labor Force Percentages		
	100 Top Concentration Areas[a]	100 Comparative Areas[a]	All Areas in the United States[b]
Agriculture	10.1	17.8	12.2
Mining	5.6	3.0	1.7
Construction	5.1	7.2	6.1
Manufacturing	38.1	19.0	25.9
Transportation, communication, and other public utilities	5.3	7.1	7.8
Wholesale and retail trade	15.0	18.2	18.8
Finance, insurance, and real estate	1.8	2.4	3.4
Business and personal services	4.5	5.8	5.8
Professional and related services	7.1	8.0	8.3
All other[c]	7.4	11.4	10.0
Total	100.0	99.9[d]	100.0

[a] U.S., Bureau of the Census, *County and City Data Book, 1952: A Supplement to the Statistical Abstract of the United States* (Washington: Government Printing Office, 1953), Table 3.
[b] *Ibid.*, Table 1.
[c] See note "d," Table 18.
[d] Rounding error.

siderable portion of the discrepancy in labor force structures as between the high concentration areas and the United
States as a whole is attributable, not to concentration differences, but to differences in the size characteristics of the areas
that make up the two groups. Similarly, Table 19 data show
that the direct comparison of labor force percentages in
"manufacturing" as between the high concentration areas
and all areas in the United States is misleading. This comparison shows the high concentration areas to contain only
about 50 per cent more workers than do all areas in the United
States. But the 50 per cent discrepancy may be thought of
as the net result of two factors—a "concentration" factor
and a "size" factor. Bringing the 100 comparative areas into
the analysis makes it clear that the concentration effect is
such as to make the manufacturing percentage almost exactly
twice as large as that in areas of lower concentration. Thus
the 100 comparative areas sample serves as a link between the
100 top area sample and the United States as a whole; its
ability to do so follows from the facts that it has size, but not
concentration, characteristics in common with the 100 top

areas and that it has concentration, but not size, characteristics in common with all areas in the United States.

Thus far the analysis has concerned the relation of concentration to the industrial composition of the total labor force in labor market areas—and thus has had reference to the first of the questions raised at the outset of this section. In what follows, the primary focus of attention is upon the industrial composition of the employment of firms that are the largest in the areas. The major aim is that of finding answers to the second and third of those questions: namely, is the industry distribution of the employment of all firms the same as that of the largest firms in labor market areas, and secondly, does the industry distribution of large-firm employment vary with the concentration position of the labor market

TABLE 20

RELATIVE FREQUENCY DISTRIBUTIONS BY SELECTED INDUSTRIES OF COVERED EMPLOYMENT[a] IN SPECIFIED NUMBERS OF FIRMS, FOR 100 TOP CONCENTRATION AREAS, 100 COMPARATIVE AREAS, AND ALL AREAS IN THE UNITED STATES

Industry	Relative Frequency Distributions						
	100 Top Areas			100 Comparative Areas			U. S., Total
	Largest Firm[b]	Four Largest Firms[b]	All Firms[c]	Largest Firm[b]	Four Largest Firms[b]	All Firms[c]	All Firms[d]
(1)	(2)	(3)	(4)	(5)	(6)	(7)	(8)
Mining	10.1	10.2	8.6	10.5	12.5	6.5	2.7
Textile mill products	24.0	21.3	12.5	6.3	7.2	2.4	3.9
Lumber and wood products	1.7	1.8	2.5	7.9	8.6	6.9	2.2
Paper and allied products	4.5	3.8	2.3	10.7	7.2	2.0	1.3
Chemicals and allied products	5.6	4.9	2.9	0.9	0.7	0.9	2.0
Primary metal industries	9.0	9.1	5.7	1.7	2.0	1.2	3.4
Machinery (except electrical)	6.3	7.0	5.9	3.3	5.3	2.2	4.3
Electrical machinery	8.2	7.2	4.4	0.7	1.1	0.5	2.4
Transportation equipment	18.4	16.7	10.2	22.4	14.0	3.5	3.6
All other	12.2	18.1	45.1	35.5	41.6	73.9	74.2
Total	100.0	100.1	100.1	99.9	100.2	100.0	100.0

[a] All data in this table are derived from BOASI sources; thus firms referred to in the table are those covered by Old-Age and Survivors Insurance in March, 1948.
[b] Source: The Time-Series Tabulation.
[c] Source: Table 615.
[d] Source: 1948 County Business Patterns, Part I, Table 1.
[e] In neither group of 100 areas is 400 firms involved. Accurate information could be obtained only for firms hiring 100 or more workers, and in many areas one or more of the four top-ranking firms hired fewer than 100 workers.

area? The data in Table 20 were obtained with these questions in mind. They consist of (a) industry percentage distributions of the employment of the largest firms, the four largest firms, and all firms of the 100 areas that ranked highest in concentration according to the summary index, (b) the same relative frequency distributions for the 100 comparative areas, and (c) a relative frequency distribution of the employment of all firms in the United States.

By way of contrasting these data with those in Tables 18 and 19, it may be noted that these data refer to a much "narrower" group of industries, and they are based solely upon 1948 BOASI data. It is clear, however, that despite these differences, they tend to support the census-derived data of Tables 18 and 19. The "all firms" columns, (4), (7), and (8), of Table 20 contain data that are comparable with the data in the three columns of Table 19. The mining percentages (of the *total* labor force) of the three groups of areas are 5.6, 3.0, and 1.7 in Table 19; in Table 20 these percentages (of the *covered* labor force) are 8.6, 6.5, and 2.7. The manufacturing percentages as shown in Table 19 are 38.1, 19.0, and 25.9; those of the eight manufacturing industries shown in Table 20 are 46.3, 19.6, and 23.1. So it is evident that these data support the census data in that they clearly indicate that high concentration areas are characterized by a disproportionate allocation of employment among certain industries.

It was found that the questions to which the data relate can most satisfactorily be approached in an order that is the reverse of that in which they were raised above. Thus the most concentrated areas were first examined to see if the *large-firm* employment was distributed disproportionately toward certain industries. The answer, as provided by columns (2) and (3) of Table 20, is very clear: 87.8 per cent of the employment of the 100 (single) largest firms and 81.9 per cent of the employment of the four largest firms in the same areas were accounted for by only nine industries. Then the 100 comparative ("low" concentration) areas were examined to see if the same nine industries accounted for different percentages of the large firm employment. As shown in columns (5) and (6) of Table 20 these industries accounted for 64.5 per cent of the total employment of the (single) largest firms and 58.4 per cent of the total employment of the four largest firms in these areas. These data, therefore, give an unequivocal answer to the question concerning the change in industrial composition of large firm employment that is associated with changes in concentration.

The other question raised at the outset of this section had to do with whether the industrial composition of the employment of large firms differs from that of all firms. Both sets of data—i.e., the 100 top areas data and the 100 comparative areas data—indicate that it does, by showing a "continuous" decrease in the proportion of total employment accounted for by the nine industries as larger numbers of firms are considered. Thus in the 100 high concentration areas the nine industries account for 87.8 per cent of the combined employment of the (single) largest firms, 81.9 per cent of that of the four largest firms, and only 54.9 per cent of that of all firms; in the 100 comparative areas the corresponding percentages are 64.5, 58.4, and 26.1.

The fact that the nine industries being investigated have their employments distributed disproportionately toward

TABLE 21

DATA WHICH DEMONSTRATE THE LARGE-FIRM CHARACTERISTICS OF THE NINE HIGH CONCENTRATION INDUSTRIES[a]

Industry	Firms This Industry as Percentage of All Firms, All Industries	Firms Hiring 100-499 Workers, This Industry, as Percentage All Firms Hiring 100-499 Workers	Firms Hiring 500 or More Workers, This Industry, as Percentage All Firms Hiring 500 or More Workers	Number Firms Hiring 100 or More Workers, This Industry, as Percentage All Firms This Industry	Average Firm Size, Employment (Arithmetic Mean)
(1)	(2)	(3)	(4)	(5)	(6)
Mining	1.1	3.6	4.5	6.0	34
Textile mill products	0.3	5.2	9.0	28.8	152
Lumber and wood products	1.5	3.4	1.3	3.4	19
Paper and allied products	0.2	2.2	2.6	25.3	111
Chemicals and allied products	0.4	2.5	3.2	10.8	64
Primary metal industries	0.2	2.6	6.0	24.2	207
Machinery (except electrical)	0.7	4.3	8.0	11.6	80
Electrical machinery	0.2	1.7	4.4	22.1	194
Transportation equipment	0.2	1.2	5.0	17.9	271
Total	4.8	26.7	44.0	—[b]	—[b]
All industries	—[b]	—[b]	—[b]	1.7	13

[a] Source: *1948 County Business Patterns*, Part I, Table 1. All firm and employment data have limitations imposed by coverage of Old-Age and Survivors Insurance Program as of March, 1948.
[b] Statistic not applicable.

large firms is demonstrated in several other ways in Table 21—a table based exclusively upon 1948 BOASI data and hence exactly comparable with the data of the preceding table. First, the disproportionate distribution is shown directly in columns (2), (3), and (4). The totals of these columns are especially revealing: they show that the nine high concentration industries account for 4.8 per cent of all covered firms, a much larger percentage, 26.7, of covered firms hiring from 100 through 499 workers, and a still larger percentage, 44.0, of the covered firms hiring 500 or more workers. Next, in column (5) the all-industry average number of firms hiring 100 or more workers is shown to be 1.7 per cent, whereas all of the nine industries under consideration here have much larger percentages—up to 28.8 per cent for "Textile mill products." Finally, in column (6) the mean employment of all covered firms is shown to be thirteen whereas the means of the nine industries are, generally, considerably higher.

In the preceding section an inverse relationship between labor force size and concentration was shown to exist. In this section it has been established that a relationship exists between concentration and industry structure and that this relationship exists when size of labor force is taken into account—that there is an industry factor in concentration that is not explained by labor force size. This leaves open the possibility that the dependence "runs in the other direction," however—that the inverse correlation observed between concentration and labor force size is "really" an industry-concentration relationship: i.e., that the small areas are higher in concentration only because they, more than large areas, tend to contain these industries.

There is evidence in two of the preceding tables bearing on this question. Consider first the portion of Table 18 labeled "All Areas by Labor Force Size." These data "say" that the labor forces of high concentration areas of all sizes are disproportionately distributed toward mining and manufacturing but that the extent of the disproportionality decreases for mining and increases for manufacturing as the labor force size of the high concentration areas increases. In other words, the mining data are consistent with the hypothesis that the community-size-concentration relationship is basically an industry-concentration relationship, but the evidence provided by the larger class, "Manufacturing," points in the opposite direction.

The same sort of information, in finer detail, can be obtained from Table 20. The two groups of 100 areas investigated there have been shown to have a small-size bias. Thus a comparison of columns (7) and (8) provides an indication as to which of the nine industries are disproportionately dis-

TABLE 22

PERCENTAGE DISTRIBUTION OF LABOR FORCES OF TWO REGIONAL GROUPINGS OF THE 100 TOP CONCENTRATION AREAS BY INDUSTRY, FOR THREE LABOR FORCE SIZE CATEGORIES

Regional Groups[a]	Percentage Distribution of Labor Force by Industry									
	Mining	Textile Mill Products	Lumber and Wood Products	Paper and Allied Products	Chemicals and Allied Products	Primary Metal Industries	Machinery, except Electrical	Electrical Machinery	Transportation Equipment	All Other
Areas Having Labor Forces of 0-5,499										
Low	8.0	3.5	37.5	13.2	0.3	6.5	0.0	0.0	0.0	30.9
High	19.7	7.9	10.3	10.0	7.7	3.4	0.2	0.0	0.0	40.8
Both	15.7	6.4	19.6	11.1	5.2	4.5	0.1	0.0	0.0	37.4
Areas Having Labor Forces of 5,500-12,499										
Low	2.7	10.9	7.4	8.5	1.3	2.1	0.6	0.0	6.7	59.7
High	14.3	15.9	2.2	4.0	8.1	4.3	5.6	0.8	3.0	41.8
Both	12.4	15.0	3.1	4.8	7.0	3.9	4.8	0.7	3.6	44.8
Areas Having Labor Forces of 12,500 and Over										
Low	10.5	20.0	1.6	1.0	6.9	7.8	3.5	3.1	0.0	45.6
High	6.2	10.3	0.6	0.6	0.3	5.8	7.6	6.5	16.2	45.9
Both	7.1	12.4	0.9	0.7	1.7	6.3	6.7	5.8	12.7	45.8
All 100 Areas										
Low	9.1	17.1	5.9	3.3	5.5	6.8	2.7	2.3	1.0	46.3
High	8.5	11.3	1.5	1.7	2.3	5.4	6.8	5.0	12.7	44.8
Both	8.6	12.5	2.5	2.3	2.9	5.7	5.9	4.4	10.2	45.1

[a] The areas in the "low" regional group are those in the regions that have regional relatives of less than 100 in Table 24, column (4)—New England, Middle Atlantic, East South Central, West South Central, Pacific. The "high" regional group consists of the areas in those which have regional relatives of 100 or more—East North Central, West North Central, South Atlantic, Mountain.

tributed toward small areas. This comparison shows that two of the eight manufacturing industries are, like "Mining," small-area industries: they are "Lumber and wood products," and "Paper and allied products." The remaining manufacturing industries, except for "Transportation equipment," appear to be distributed in the other direction. Moving on across the table, from right to left, makes it possible to observe supplementary information. Comparing columns (7)-(6)-(5) with (4)-(3)-(2) shows the industry-concentration relationship; combining this with the (8)-(7) comparison reveals that the industry-concentration relationship is weakest in the three industries most heavily distributed toward small areas.[11]

Additional evidence on the question of whether there is or is not an independent community-size-concentration effect may be seen in Table 22. There the relative frequency distribution of the employed labor forces of the 100 top concentration areas is presented by community-size categories. (For purposes of this discussion the relevant data are found in the rows labeled "both"; reference will be made to the "high" and "low" regional group classes in the following section.) The results clarify to some extent the picture that was emerging in the above two paragraphs. It has previously been shown that the 100 top concentration areas are distributed almost uniformly throughout the size range of all 1,774 labor market areas; the small size bias of these areas derives from their over-representation among the very small areas and under-representation in the few very largest ones. Table 22 shows that the industrial composition of high concentration areas varies quite substantially with labor force size. Thus the two manufacturing industries previously shown to be distributed especially toward small areas, "lumber" and "paper," are seen here to account for almost one-third of the labor force of the areas in the "0-5,499" size class but less than 2 per cent of the labor force of those areas in the "12,500 and over" size class. Correspondingly, three manufacturing industries ("machinery," "electrical machinery," and "transportation equipment") accounting for one-fourth of the labor force of the areas in the "12,500 and over" class almost fail to appear in the "0-5,499" class. The other four

11. Two reservations about the use of the comparative sample in this and the preceding paragraph are mentioned in the concluding paragraph of Section 15 of the Appendix.

industries have important labor force components in all size classes, but there are strong inclinations in two of them: "mining" toward small areas and "textiles" toward large.

The evidence cited in the preceding three paragraphs does not clearly resolve the question at issue: Is the community-size-concentration relationship "really" an industry-concentration relationship? Certain of the high concentration industries seem to be distributed especially in the direction of small areas and thus tend to give an affirmative answer to the question. But others clearly are distributed disproportionately *away from* small areas and, by producing high concentration in large areas, tend to establish a *positive* correlation between community size and concentration. Still others seem to be distributed in such a way as to exercise no large effect in either of these directions. It does appear, however, that the industries distributed predominately toward larger areas account for larger percentages of the employed labor forces in high concentration areas—as shown by column (4) in Table 20 or the bottom row of Table 22; this favors the conclusion that the industry-concentration relationship does not underlie that between concentration and community size.[12]

An effort to get more directly at the question under discussion consisted of the following brief experiment. The 100 high concentration areas were classified according to the ten industry groups of Tables 20 and 22, the nine high concentration industries plus "all others." Classification was based on industry of the largest firm. For each of the nine industries, rank correlation coefficients were computed for rankings by community size and concentration. The results, presented in Table 23, must be used with care, for the numbers of observations are small and the classification by industry is crude. Within their restricted sphere of meaning, however, they support the notion that the concentration-community-size relationship exists independently of the concentration-industry relationship; six of the nine coefficients are negative, and the industries with the largest numbers of areas—"mining" and "textiles"—are among the six.

12. The "All Regions" part of Table 28 in the following section provides means of allocating employment of high concentration industries between small and large areas for the United States as a whole. Despite the fact that only standard metropolitan areas are classified as "large areas" in that table, the employment of the nine high concentration industries is distributed disproportionately toward "large areas"—thus supporting the conclusion in the text above.

TABLE 23

RANK CORRELATION COEFFICIENTS BETWEEN CONCENTRATION[a]
AND COMMUNITY SIZE[b] FOR 100 HIGH CONCENTRATION
AREAS WITHIN INDUSTRY CLASSES

Industry[c]	Number of Areas	Coefficient[d]
Mining	18	−.46
Textile mill products	18	−.23
Lumber and wood products	7	+.14
Paper and allied products	9	−.38
Chemicals and allied products	6	+.14
Primary metal industries	8	−.29
Machinery (except electrical)	5	−.90
Electrical machinery	5	+.80
Transportation equipment	6	−.77
All other[e]	18	—[e]

[a] The measure used for ranking areas by concentration was Overall-1.
[b] The Overall denominator was used as the ranking measure for community size.
[c] Areas were classified by industry according to the industry of the largest firm.
[d] The numbers in this column are Spearman rank correlation coefficients.
[e] Seventeen areas had largest firms outside the nine high concentration industries; a coefficient was not computed for these areas. The other area in this class belongs in "Textile mill products"; since, however, the employment of the largest firm in this area had to be estimated by a method that could have caused serious overstatement—thus causing its Overall-1 concentration ratio to be too large—it was omitted from the rank coefficient computations.

By way of brief summary of the above industry findings, these statements appear to be warranted. The industrial distribution of the labor forces of highly concentrated areas is different from that of other areas in that relatively larger proportions of the labor forces of these areas are associated with mining and manufacturing. Nine industries—mining and eight manufacturing industries—account for approximately 45 per cent of the employed labor force of all covered firms within the 100 areas highest in concentration and approximately 88 per cent of the labor force of the 100 largest firms in these areas. These industries also account for an abnormally large proportion of the labor forces of the largest firms in areas that are not highly concentrated, but the proportion is smaller. More generally, they may be described as "large firm" industries in the sense that employment in them is distributed relatively more heavily toward large firms. It does not appear that the industrial aspects of concentration account for the inverse correlation between labor force size and concentration. It is evident, however, that size and industry are related; the industrial distribution of the labor force of high concentration areas shifts appreciably among the nine industries with changes in labor force size.

TABLE 24

A COMPARISON OF THE REGIONAL DISTRIBUTION OF THE LABOR
FORCE IN THE 100 MOST CONCENTRATED AREAS
AND IN ALL 1,774 AREAS

| Region | Percentage of Labor Force | | Regional Relatives: Col. (2) × 100/ Col. (3) |
| | 100 Top Areas | All Areas | |
(1)	(2)	(3)	(4)
New England	2.8	7.0	40
Middle Atlantic	6.8	22.6	30
East North Central	39.6	22.0	180
West North Central	9.9	7.4	134
South Atlantic	22.7	12.3	185
East South Central	6.4	6.5	98
West South Central	4.4	8.5	52
Mountain	5.2	2.7	193
Pacific	2.2	11.1	20

7. CONCENTRATION AND GEOGRAPHIC REGION

The purely descriptive questions: "Do the areas in some regions tend to have greater concentration than the areas in other regions?" and "Does employment of high concentration areas tend to have a different regional distribution than low concentration areas?" can be answered rather readily. Table 24 shows the regional distribution of the labor force of the 100 areas that ranked highest on the summary index C' in comparison with the regional distribution of the labor force of all 1,774 areas. It will be noted that the labor force of the 100 most concentrated areas falls disproportionately in the East North Central, the South Atlantic, the Mountain, and, to a lesser extent, the West North Central regions relative to the regional distribution of the labor force of all of the areas.

Table 24 is concerned primarily with the 100 most concentrated areas. To obtain Table 25 all 1,774 areas were ranked by concentration using Maximum-4 as the index of concentration. They were divided into ten concentration classes, and the labor force in each concentration class was then distributed by region; regional cumulative relative frequency distributions were computed and are presented in the columns of the table. These distributions are measures of regional concentration in that they indicate the proportions of the regional labor forces in various concentration rank categories. For example, the top row of the table shows the labor force proportions of the regions in the top-ranking 177

TABLE 25

REGIONAL CUMULATIVE RELATIVE FREQUENCY DISTRIBUTIONS OF
LABOR FORCE BY CONCENTRATION RANK (MAXIMUM-4
INDEX) OF LABOR MARKET AREA

Areas Ranking	Percentage of Regional Labor Force in Concentration Rank Class								
	New England	Middle Atlantic	East North Central	West North Central	South Atlantic	East South Central	West South Central	Mountain	Pacific
177 and above	1.6	2.2	5.6	4.0	8.6	4.3	2.5	11.9	1.2
354 and above	4.9	4.1	16.6	6.9	17.2	15.3	6.0	15.1	1.7
531 and above	6.1	6.8	24.1	10.7	21.9	23.9	7.9	18.2	3.0
709 and above	16.5	11.3	23.0	15.4	29.8	33.8	11.3	21.6	3.3
886 and above	21.5	15.9	39.4	19.9	37.3	40.4	12.9	24.3	4.1
1,064 and above	28.9	18.7	43.9	25.8	45.8	51.2	18.5	28.1	6.1
1,241 and above	35.0	22.5	59.3	31.4	54.3	58.1	24.6	34.6	16.8
1,419 and above	48.5	25.1	67.1	44.9	71.0	74.0	31.5	38.9	19.9
1,596 and above	55.8	38.5	70.2	56.9	85.0	88.9	46.2	62.7	22.3
1,774 and above	100.0	100.0	100.0	100.0	100.0	100.0	100.0	100.0	100.0

areas; the fact that a regional ranking according to this row
would be very similar to a ranking based on the regional
relatives computed for the top 100 areas (as shown in Table
24) indicates that the pattern of regional concentration as
established by the 100 top concentration areas is only slightly
disturbed by consideration of the next seventy-seven areas, in
regard to rank. In fact, it is clear that this basic pattern
remains largely as established by the top 100 areas throughout the table, except that the Mountain region slips from the
top to about the middle of the ranks and the East South Central does substantially the reverse.

The questions that were raised at the outset and the answers that are provided in Tables 24 and 25 are descriptive
ones. It is well known that the average size of community
differs substantially among regions and also that there are
large differences in the industrial composition of the labor
forces of different regions. The two preceding sections have
pointed out that small communities tend to be more concentrated than large ones and that the industrial composition of
the labor force of high concentration communities is not the
same as that for low concentration communities. The remainder of this section will, therefore, be concerned with
answering this analytical question: Do these two factors
"explain" the observed regional variation in concentration?

That is, are the regions that rank high in concentration simply those that tend to have small communities and high concentration industries?

The data of Table 26, part of Table 22, and Table 28 were gathered for this purpose. First, the 1,774 areas were classified by region and size (of labor force); then the mean and median of Maximum-4 concentration ratios and the percentage of regional labor force were found for each of these region-size classes. These data, presented in Table 26, were designed primarily to provide comparisons of the concentration position of the nine regions within community size classes.

The first and most obvious contribution of the data in the table is their clear reaffirmation of the inverse concentration-community-size relationship, expressed in the bottom "All regions" row of data; both means and medians decrease as

TABLE 26

MEDIANS AND MEANS OF CONCENTRATION RATIOS AND LABOR FORCE PERCENTAGES OF AREAS IN SPECIFIED REGIONS AND OF SPECIFIED AREA SIZES (MAXIMUM-4 INDEXES USED THROUGHOUT)

Region	Size of Labor Force Area											
	0-6,999			7,000-14,999			15,000 and Over			All Sizes		
	Median	Mean	Percentage of Regional Labor Force	Median	Mean	Percentage of Regional Labor Force	Median	Mean	Percentage of Regional Labor Force	Median	Mean	Percentage of Regional Labor Force
(1)	(2)	(3)	(4)	(5)	(6)	(7)	(8)	(9)	(10)	(11)	(12)	(13)
New England	26	41	1	27	30	5	21	21	94	23	26	100
Middle Atlantic	30	32	0[a]	23	25	3	21	24	97	23	25	100
East North Central	25	28	4	25	27	13	30	31	83	26	29	100
West North Central	23	25	11	16	21	25	15	21	64	19	23	100
South Atlantic	25	31	9	25	29	23	20	24	68	24	28	100
East South Central	26	30	14	24	26	30	20	23	56	24	27	100
West South Central	25	31	6	14	19	20	10	12	74	14	20	100
Mountain	29	41	17	14	21	25	11	19	58	22	32	100
Pacific	32	37	2	16	19	5	8	15	93	17	23	100
All regions	25	31	5	21	25	13	18	23	82	—[b]	—[b]	100

[a] Less than one-half of 1 per cent.
[b] Statistic not computed.

community size increases. Beyond this, the regional relative distributions of the labor force among community size categories are quite helpful, for it is apparent by observation that these distributions are related to regional concentration. For example, the three regions (New England, Middle Atlantic, and Pacific) which, according to column 10, Table 26, have the largest percentages of their labor forces in the large community size category, are also the three regions that show the smallest three relatives in column 4, Table 24. More exactly, the rank correlation coefficient relating regional ranks according to column 4 of Table 24 and those according to the sum of columns 4 and 7 of Table 26 is plus .68. This indicates that the differences in the distribution of regional labor forces among labor market areas of various sizes constitutes a part of the explanation of regional concentration differences.

Variation in the regional averages (means and medians) of concentration ratios *within* these size categories could come about as a result of industry factors, other systematic factors, regional factors—if there are any such—and random factors. Distinguishing among these influences is complicated by the disproportionate labor force content (82 per cent) of the third community size category; its averages are not weighted, so it presents problems of interpretation similar to those of Table 14. That is, the averages of the regions in which large proportions of workers live—in and around metropolitan areas—are surely "too high"; hence the averages shown in the large community size category of the table should be adjusted downward in amounts functionally related to the percentages of column 10.

However, there does seem to be an industry influence that shows through the Table 26 data in their present form. The classes provided there give regional rankings from which the community size determinant has been "removed." Within these classes New England and the Middle Atlantic states consistently rank high in concentration; yet both rank low in Tables 24 and 25. These two regions are heavily endowed with many of the high concentration industries—as can be seen in Tables 28 and 29. It is a reasonable presumption, in the light of the findings of the preceding section, that their high rank positions within community size classes are related to industry structure. It would be hazardous to try to go beyond this point in explaining regional concentration on the basis of the evidence in this table.

In the preceding section, Table 22 was used as a means of analyzing change in industrial structure among three community size categories of the 100 high concentration areas. The portions of the table not used in that analysis were the "high" and "low" rows, which break the areas within the community size categories into two groups: those that are located in regions ranking "high" in Table 24 and those which are located in regions ranking "low" in Table 24. Thus the sub-classes were designed to indicate whether there were industrial differences that might help explain regional rankings. The question to be answered is this: To what extent are there industry uniformities among the three "low" distributions that contrast with comparable similarities among the "high" distributions? If the data show no such uniformities among the "high" and "low" distributions, or if they do show such uniformities but these uniformities do not differ as between the "high" and "low" distributions, the inference of the data is that industry structure is not a factor in the explanation of regional concentration differences.[13]

In fact, the data show industry uniformities some of which are, and some of which are not, shared by "high" and "low" regions. Thus there are nine industries under observation: three of these ("mining," "textile mill products," and "primary metal products") are of relatively great importance in the areas of both "high" and "low" regions; three of the industries ("lumber and wood products," "paper and allied products," and "chemicals and allied products") tend to be relatively more important in the "low" regions than in the "high"; and three of the industries ("machinery, except electrical," "electrical machinery," and "transportation equipment") tend to be relatively more important in the "high" regions than in the "low." Thus the data definitely suggest that variation in the distribution of the high concentration industries among regions is a part of the explanation of regional variation in concentration.

13. The point being made here is that the analysis should start by a check upon whether different industries account for the high concentration areas of the two groups of regions. This leaves open the possibility that the same industries are responsible for high concentration in both sets of regions but that these industries are more heavily distributed toward the high concentration set; this matter will receive further attention in connection with Table 28.

In the preceding section it was observed from Table 22 data that certain industries were more important in the smaller of the high concentration areas, certain others were more important in the areas of all size groups, and still others were more important in the larger areas. It is interesting to note that these three groupings correspond almost exactly with those of the preceding paragraph. Thus "electrical machinery," "machinery, except electrical," and "transportation equipment" are the industries the relative importance of which increases as area size increases, and they are also the three industries that are of greatest importance in the "high" regional group. Similarly, three of the four industries that suffer a decline in importance among the top concentration areas as "size" increases ("lumber and wood products," "paper and allied products," and "chemicals and allied products") are industries that are of greatest comparative importance in the "low" regional group of areas. Significantly, these three industries rank seventh, eighth, and ninth among the nine high concentration industries in the number of very large (500 employees and over) firms contained, as shown in Table 21, column 4. The impression cre-

TABLE 27

THE 100 HIGH CONCENTRATION AREAS DISTRIBUTED BY REGION AND INDUSTRY[a]

Region	Number of Areas										
	Mining	Textile Mill Products[b]	Lumber and Wood Products	Paper and Allied Products	Chemicals and Allied Products	Primary Metal Industries	Machinery (except Electrical)	Electrical Machinery	Transportation Equipment	All Other	Total
New England	—	2	—	—	—	—	—	—	—	—	2
Middle Atlantic	2	1	—	—	1	—	—	1	—	—	5
East North Central	1	—	—	—	1	1	2	4	5	4	18
West North Central	1	—	—	2	—	1	3	—	—	3	10
South Atlantic	3	14	1	5	3	—	—	—	—	3	29
East South Central	1	2	—	—	—	2	—	—	1	2	8
West South Central	—	—	2	2	—	—	—	—	—	3	7
Mountain	10	—	1	—	—	4	—	—	—	2	17
Pacific	—	—	3	—	1	—	—	—	—	—	4

[a] Areas were classified by industry according to the industry of the largest firm.
[b] This table shows 19 high concentration areas in "Textile mill products" whereas Table 23, using the same system of classification and the same 100 areas, shows 18. The discrepancy is explained in note "e" to that table.

ated by these observations is that the high concentration regions are those with a "heavy" industry base. But this clearly is not a fully satisfactory conclusion, for Table 24 rates the Middle Atlantic states low and the Mountain states high.

The data in Table 27 add perspective to the preceding explorations. Here the relationship between concentration and region can be seen easily in the last column, "Total": the regions that have been specified as high concentration regions primarily on percentage-of-labor-force criteria, are seen to be those which contain large numbers of highly concentrated labor markets. Looking further, the influence of "industry" is apparent—but it is a more complicated influence than suggested by the preceding paragraph. Just as earlier analysis disclosed that concentration involved labor market areas of "all" sizes—rather than, say, only those of small size—so this investigation shows that "all" of the high concentration industries are involved in the different regional rankings, with quite different industrial patterns being associated with different regions. Thus the conclusion of the preceding paragraph is seen to refer primarily to the East North Central region; its high concentration position is indeed based squarely on the "heavy" end of the industrial complex. But the high concentration position of the South Atlantic region is based upon industries that are distributed more toward small- and intermediate-size areas, whereas that of the Mountain states is based almost exclusively on metal extraction and processing.

Table 28 is based on 1950 Census information. It is a regional distribution of employed workers of the nine high concentration industries, and "all other" industries, by community size. The "large" areas of the table are standard metropolitan areas; the "small" areas are all areas outside standard metropolitan area boundaries. Thus the beginning of the "mining" row of data shows that New England contained 0.5 per cent of the total employed labor force in mining in 1950—0.2 per cent in large areas and 0.3 per cent in small areas. Comparison of these three figures with the three immediately above them—the percentages of the total ("All Industries") employed labor force in the New England categories—provides an indication as to whether this region has an "abnormally" large or small proportion of these workers,

TABLE 28.   PERCENTAGE DISTRIBUTION OF EMPLOYED
REGION AND BY COMMUNITY

Industry	Percentage of Industry Total Employment by Region[a]														
	New England			Middle Atlantic			East North Central			West North Central			South Atlantic		
	Total	Large Areas	Small Areas	Total	Large Areas	Small Areas	Total	Large Areas	Small Areas	Total	Large Areas	Small Areas	Total	Large Areas	Small Areas
All Industries	6.4	4.2	2.2	21.0	17.6	3.4	21.1	13.0	8.1	9.5	4.0	5.5	13.6	6.1	7.5
Mining	0.5	0.2	0.3	22.1	11.4	10.7	11.6	1.3	10.3	5.2	1.7	3.5	19.5	4.2	15.3
Textile mill products	21.0	11.8	9.2	23.6	19.1	4.5	3.8	2.5	1.3	0.7	0.5	0.2	40.7	8.6	32.1
Lumber and wood products	5.0	0.7	4.3	5.4	2.8	2.6	9.0	2.5	6.5	3.7	1.2	2.5	25.6	3.2	22.4
Paper and allied products	14.3	6.5	7.8	25.9	20.1	5.8	27.8	14.3	13.5	4.3	3.2	1.1	10.6	4.6	6.0
Chemicals and allied products	4.7	3.9	0.8	29.6	26.3	3.3	21.2	15.6	5.6	5.0	4.1	0.9	17.3	10.0	7.3
Primary metal industries	4.9	3.9	1.0	33.1	28.5	4.6	38.9	29.8	9.1	2.9	3.3	-0.4d	5.8	6.5	-0.7d
Machinery, except electrical	11.0	7.7	3.3	21.9	17.4	4.5	47.4	33.4	14.0	7.1	6.3	0.8	2.4	1.5	0.9
Electrical machinery	12.7	9.4	3.3	37.0	32.4	4.6	37.4	27.5	9.9	4.7	4.2	0.5	2.5	1.9	0.6
Transportation equipment	4.3	3.2	1.1	15.0	13.9	1.1	55.6	46.2	9.4	4.0	3.7	0.3	5.0	3.7	1.3
All other industries	6.0	4.0	2.0	20.7	17.5	3.2	19.5	11.5	8.0	10.5	4.2	6.3	13.5	6.4	7.1

[a] There are two community size classes in the table, "large" areas and "small" areas. The large areas are standard metropolitan areas; the small areas are all areas not included within standard metropolitan areas (as defined for purposes of the 1950 Census).

[b] Source: U.S., Bureau of the Census, *1950 Census of Population: Detailed Characteristics*, Preprint of Volume II, Chapter C. All data computed from tables 70 and 130.

in total and by community size. For example, comparing the total "Mining" and "All Industries" percentages makes it clear that mining employment is not distributed disproportionately toward New England; that region contains 6.4 per cent of the total employed labor force but only 0.5 per cent of the total employed labor force in mining.[14]

The preceding analysis has shown that both community size and "industry" factors contributed to regional concentration variation. The question that remains unresolved is this: Do these factors account for *all* regional variation? Or: If the data could be "perfectly" standardized for the two factors known to be important, would there still be "unexplained" *systematic* variation of a regional character?

Clearly, Table 28 does not give a direct answer to these queries. However, in conjunction with data in the other tables, it makes possible experiments that might suggest the

14. It was noted in the preceding section that Table 20 shows three of the nine high concentration industries ("mining," "lumber," and "paper") to be distributed toward small areas. The "All Regions" portion of Table 28 provides more accurate information of this type, and it confirms the Table 20 indication. Table 28 suggests that "textiles" should be added to the list; this undoubtedly is a result of the fact that its "small areas" are much larger, on average, than those of Table 20. (See the following footnote.) Table 28 designates "transportation equipment" as a "large areas" industry; this surely is a more accurate classification than that provided by Table 20.

LABOR FORCE IN HIGH CONCENTRATION INDUSTRIES BY
SIZE[a] WITHIN REGIONS[b]

| Percentage of Industry Total Employment by Region[c] | | | | | | | | | | | | | | |
| East South Central | | | West South Central | | | Mountain | | | Pacific | | | All Regions | | |
Total	Large Areas	Small Areas	Total	Large Areas	Small Areas	Total	Large Areas	Small Areas	Total	Large Areas	Small Areas	Total	Large Areas	Small Areas
6.8	2.1	4.7	8.9	3.5	5.4	3.1	0.8	2.3	9.5	7.0	2.5	100.0	58.4	41.6
12.4	2.2	10.2	17.3	3.7	13.6	7.6	0.7	6.9	3.9	1.7	2.2	100.0	27.0	73.0
7.9	1.9	6.0	1.2	0.5	0.7	0.3	0.1	0.2	0.9	0.8	0.1	100.0	45.8	54.2
15.4	2.2	13.2	12.2	1.3	10.9	2.7	0.2	2.5	21.0	4.5	16.5	100.0	18.6	81.4
4.1	1.8	2.3	5.6	1.8	3.8	0.3	0.2	0.1	7.2	5.0	2.2	100.0	57.4	42.6
7.8	4.1	3.7	7.2	3.3	3.9	1.0	0.6	0.4	6.2	4.8	1.4	100.0	72.7	27.3
5.8	3.6	2.2	2.1	1.2	0.9	2.6	0.5	2.1	4.1	3.9	0.2	100.0	81.2	18.8
2.0	1.4	0.6	2.9	2.0	0.9	0.6	0.4	0.2	4.6	4.2	0.4	100.0	74.3	25.7
1.3	0.4	0.9	0.8	0.6	0.2	0.2	0.1	0.1	3.4	3.3	0.1	100.0	79.9	20.1
1.1	0.7	0.4	2.9	2.3	0.6	0.2	0.1	0.1	12.0	11.2	0.8	100.0	84.8	15.2
6.9	2.1	4.8	9.6	3.8	5.8	3.4	0.9	2.4	9.9	7.4	2.5	100.0	57.8	42.2

[c] The word "region" in this table corresponds with the census term "division."
[d] These negative figures result from the treatment given certain standard metropolitan areas that are on the border of geographic regions, overlapping two or more of them. For purposes of this table such standard metropolitan areas were not divided, but were included within one region—a fact that makes it possible for the number of workers in an industry in the regional standard metropolitan areas to exceed the combined number of workers in that same industry in the states of the region.

presence or absence of systematic regional variation not accounted for by size or industry factors. For example, if region "A" shows higher concentration than region "B," yet clearly has consistently larger labor market areas and proportionately fewer of the nine industries that have been shown to be especially important in concentration, the implication is that community size and industry do not completely explain concentration—that there is some other factor influencing the regional results. If this sort of result occurs only occasionally, it might be concluded that random elements entered the picture or that the crudeness of the measures was responsible. If it occurs frequently, however, one is led toward the belief that previously unrecognized systematic elements are involved.

Table 25 provides means of ranking regions by concentration. Any of the rows of data in the table, except the bottom one, can serve this purpose, the differences in the rankings obviously reflecting the differences in the total number of areas brought into the ranking measures. Since the industry-regional data of Table 28 relate to all areas, perhaps the most appropriate row of Table 25 data for present purposes is the one that is next to the bottom, labeled "1,596 and above." Regions are ranked by the proportions of their labor forces which are in this category: thus the East South Central region ranks highest with 88.9 per cent of its labor force in this class and the Pacific region ranks ninth with only 22.3 per cent of its labor force in this class.

Experiment 1: Consider the West North Central and West South Central regions, which have the "same" (5.5 and 5.4 per cent, respectively) percentages of total labor force in small areas according to Table 28. The West North Central region has no disproportionate distribution of any of the high concentration industries, whereas the West South Central region has a disproportionate distribution of two of these industries. This combination of factors suggests that the West South Central region should rank higher according to concentration, if there is no other major concentration influence. According to the "1,596 and above" row of Table 25, however, the West North Central region's concentration position exceeds that of the West South Central region. This result suggests another concentration influence. However, it can be seen that an alternative explanation may lie in the community size measure. Thus, if the sum of columns 4 and 7 of Table 26 (which sum shows the percentage of regional labor force in areas having employed labor forces of 15,000 or less) is used as the measure, the two regions do not have the same community size characteristics at all. The labor force of the West North Central region is distributed more toward the especially small areas; and its higher concentration position can be reconciled with the data by "assuming" that its lesser industry position is more than offset, concentration-wise, by its greater proportion of small areas.

Experiment 2: Consider the Mountain and New England regions; they have "the same" community size characteristics, as shown by their aggregate small areas percentages in Table 28: 2.3 and 2.2, respectively. The disproportionate presence of high concentration industries in the small areas of New England is vastly greater than that of the Mountain region. However, according to the "1,596 and above" row of measures in Table 25, the Mountain region is characterized by higher concentration than is New England. Again however, this result can be reconciled by examination of the sum of columns 4 and 7 of Table 26: the percentage of regional labor force in areas with less than 15,000 employed workers is 42 for the Mountain region and only 6 for New England.

Experiment 3: This experiment was designed to retest the phenomena of the first two experiments. Consider the New England and Pacific regions; they have approximately the same percentage of labor force in small areas according to Table 28; in this case, however, the Table 26 small areas percentages are also in agreement. New England, according to Table 28, has a greater disproportionate distribution of the high concentration industries. These factors suggest that New England should occupy a higher rank position than does the Pacific region; and, as Table 25 shows, it does.

These three experiments suggest very strongly that the sum of columns 4 and 7 of Table 26 is a better measure of the community size factor than is the small-areas percentage of Table 28.[15] The results less strongly suggest that the percentage of labor force in small areas is a more forceful determinant of regional concentration than is the disproportionate location of the nine high concentration industries. Other regional comparisons along lines of the above experiments can be made which support these conclusions. The evidence presented thus far is not sufficient, however, to permit a judgment as to whether community size and industry together offer a "complete" explanation of regional concentration.

The following experiments use the measures presented in Table 29; these measures are indicators of concentration, community size, and the disproportionate distribution of high concentration industries toward small areas. The concentration measure is the one drawn from Table 25 ("1,596 and

15. There are important differences between these two measures. First, the Table 28 measure includes much larger areas: it encompasses 42 per cent of the total labor force whereas the Table 26 measure includes only 18 per cent. (See the "All Regions"·"Small Areas"·"All Industries" statistic in Table 28, and the sum of the "All Regions" statistics for columns 4 and 7 in Table 26.) Second, Table 28 refers to the whole United States labor force, whereas Table 26 includes only the labor force of the 1,774 areas covered by this study. This means that the Table 26 indicator gives community size information about the same areas to which the concentration indicator refers. The Table 28 measure gives community size information about a broader universe; its larger scope is especially important in this connection because the additional coverage consists, for all practical purposes, only of labor market areas with quite small labor forces. Finally, the Table 28 measures show, for each region, the percentage of the *total U.S. labor force* in the small areas of that region; the Table 26 measures show, for each region, the percentage of the *regional labor force* within the small areas of that region.

TABLE 29

REGIONAL MEASURES OF CONCENTRATION AND OF TWO FACTORS
INFLUENCING THE LEVEL OF CONCENTRATION:
"COMMUNITY SIZE" AND "INDUSTRY"

Region (1)	Measures		
	Concentration[a] (2)	"Community Size"[b] (3)	"Industry"[c] (4)
New England	56	6	157
Middle Atlantic	39	3	136
East North Central	70	17	109
West North Central	57	36	19
South Atlantic	85	32	126
East South Central	89	44	94
West South Central	46	26	73
Mountain	63	42	61
Pacific	22	7	106

[a] Concentration: Table 25, row "1,596 and above." These measures show the percentage of regional employed labor force found in the top-ranking 90 per cent of all 1,774 areas.
[b] "Community Size": Table 26, columns (4) and (7). These measures show the percentage of regional labor force in that 70 per cent of all 1,774 areas with labor forces of less than 15,000. Thus the *larger* the measures in this column, the *smaller* the general level of community size.
[c] "Industry." Computed from Table 28 *for each region* as follows: the small-area, all-industry percentage was divided into the nine small-area, individual industry percentages; each was multiplied by 100; the resulting relatives were summed and divided by 900.

above") and the community size measure is the sum of
columns 4 and 7 of Table 26. (Thus the *larger* the numbers
in the community size column, the *smaller* the "average"
labor market in the region; that is, the larger numbers in the
column indicate a greater tendency for the regional labor
force to be distributed toward the smaller areas.) The "industry" measure was computed from Table 28 as follows:
nine industry relatives were computed *for each region* by
dividing the percentage of industry employment in small
areas by the all-industry percentage employment in small
areas and multiplying the results by 100. For example, the
New England relatives were computed by dividing 0.3 by 2.2,
9.2 by 2.2, 4.3 by 2.2, etc., and multiplying each of the resulting
nine figures by 100. The sum of these relatives divided by
900 thus provides a crude measure of the extent to which the
nine high concentration industries are distributed disproportionately toward the not-large areas of the nine regions.

Experiment 4: The Mountain region has the "same" community size measure as does the East South Central region
(42 vs. 44) but a lower "industry" index (61 vs. 94); these
factors suggest that concentration should be lower in the
Mountain region than in the East South Central region, and

it is (63 vs. 89). Other experiments of this sort—i.e., in which community size is "held constant"—show a consistent coincidence of "predicted" and "realized" relationships between the industry and concentration measures.

Experiment 5: The West South Central and Mountain regions have the "same" industry indexes (73 vs. 61); but the West South Central region community size measure is less than that of the Mountain region (26 vs. 42). These measures would lead to the prediction that the concentration index of the West South Central region would be lower than that of the Mountain region, and it is (46 vs. 63). Again, similar experiments—with industry "held constant"—provide comparable results.

Experiment 6: The New England and the West North Central regions have the "same" concentration indexes (56 vs. 57). There is an *inverse* relationship between their community size and industry measures; that is, the New England industry index is considerably greater than that of the West North Central region (157 vs. 19) whereas the relationship between the community size measures is just the opposite (New England, 6; West North Central, 36). Similarly, comparisons of other pairs of regions with the "same" concentration indexes show the same inverse relationship between the community size and industry measures.

Experiment 7: Finally a multiple correlation coefficient was computed from the measures in Table 29; community size and industry were the independent variables, concentration was the dependent variable. In view of the results of the immediately-preceding experiments the coefficient of plus .893 is not surprising. The partial coefficients were plus .893 (concentration vs. community size) and plus .790 (concentration vs. industry). In addition, a simple correlation coefficient between the independent measures was computed. It was minus .669.[16]

16. Another set of coefficients was computed which was based upon the Table 29 data as shown in the text, except that a different set of community size measures was used. The substitute measures were obtained from Table 28 by dividing, for each region, the "Total" figure of the "All Industries" row into the "Small Areas" figure of the same row. (Thus getting rid of the third of the three differences pointed to in the preceding footnote.) The multiple coefficient of correlation was plus .774, and the partial coefficients were plus .774 (concentration vs. community size) and plus .598 (concentration vs. industry). This computation served as a check on the other correlation results and upon the judgment that the Table 26 community size measures were preferable to those obtained from Table 28.

These experiments combine to create a strong presumption against there being any systematic variation in the concentration data other than community size and industry. It is difficult to believe that the "predicted" results would so consistently have been realized or that the multiple and partial correlation coefficients would have been so high if there had been other important sources of systematic regional variation. Moreover, the evidences of a powerful inverse concentration-community-size relationship when industry is "held constant" and the inverse relationship between community size and industry suggests the answer to the question raised in Section 5: the community-size-concentration relationship was not clearly apparent except among the very large and very small areas (where its strength was greatest) because of the influence of the industry-concentration relationship.

8. SUMMARY

This chapter has consisted of a detailed presentation and analysis of the concentration ratios for 1,774 labor market areas. The data have been examined with a view toward gaining insights into the absolute level of concentration and its firm size, labor force size, industry, and regional characteristics. The results of the analysis will be summarized in detail in Chapter IV.

SUMMARY AND CONCLUSIONS

This study is directed toward an understanding of the extent of monopsonistic behavior within the unskilled and semi-skilled sectors of local labor markets. The basic data are called concentration ratios, six of which were computed for each of 1,774 labor market areas; they show the extent to which employment is concentrated within one or a few firms. The theoretical relationship between market structure (as indicated by measures such as these) and monopsonistic behavior may be stated in this way: the payment of wages less than those that would be paid under competitive conditions is most likely to occur in those labor markets in which a few employers hire a large proportion of the workers. The reasoning underlying this hypothesis is that effective monopsonistic activity requires collusion among buyers, that collusion is costly, that the cost is directly related to the number of participants in the collusive action, and that, therefore, the cost-gains relationship becomes more favorable as the degree of concentration increases (as the number of firms required to achieve any given level of concentration decreases), other things (primarily, labor supply conditions) being the same.

Most of the 1,774 labor market areas are single counties, but some comprise two or more counties that were combined to avoid large-scale commuting error. All counties having at least one firm that was covered by the OASI program in March, 1948, and that had 100 or more employees at that time are included. The use of this 100 employee criterion brought approximately 93 per cent of the employed labor force into the field of inquiry. Since the size of the largest firms of highly concentrated areas proves typically to be quite large—

the mean employment size of firms ranking first in the areas comprising the top 10 per cent of all 1,774 areas was 2,523—the possibility that many labor markets of high monopsonistic potential were omitted is not great. Rather, it seems probable that these omissions exert a conservative influence on the total body of data—that the data show a higher general level of concentration than would have been shown had all counties in the United States been included.

The complete concentration situation in any labor market area may be expressed graphically by means of the concentration curve—a curve showing cumulative percentages of employed workers hired by successively larger numbers of firms, when those firms have been arrayed from large to small. The concentration ratios of this study may be thought of as two separate estimates for each of three points on the concentration curves of all 1,774 areas; the three points are those of the one, four, and ten largest firms. One of the sets of three points—called Overall concentration ratios—consists of the summed employment of the largest, the four largest, and the ten largest firms, each expressed as a ratio to an estimate of the total employed labor force. It is quite likely, however, that these ratios, which have *total* firm figures in their numerators and *total* labor force figures as denominators, understate the degree of concentration in the not-skilled portion of the market, because of the tendency of large firms to employ larger percentages of not-skilled workers than small firms; the degree of this understatement was roughly estimated to be 16 per cent. So another set of measures was devised which err in the direction of overstatement. These measures, called Maximum concentration ratios, are exactly like the Overall ratios except that the professional, entrepreneurial, managerial, skilled, and agricultural workers have been deleted from the denominators—the numerators are the same. The deleted components comprised approximately 43 per cent of the 1950 labor force, so the Maximum measures tend, on the average, to be approximately 75 per cent larger than their Overall counterparts. Thus the two types of ratios probably bracket the corresponding "true" ratios in such a way that the real-world concentration curves lie much closer to the Overall curves than to the Maximum curves.

The numerators of the concentration ratios were obtained directly from OASI tabulations of employers' first quarter

TABLE 30

PERCENTAGE OF AREAS THE CONCENTRATION RATIOS
OF WHICH ARE UNDER 50 PER CENT[a]

Number of Firms	Type of Concentration Measure	
	Maximum	Overall
1	97.7	99.7
4	91.3	98.9
10	81.3	97.8

[a] Source: Table 4.

TABLE 31

PERCENTAGE OF LABOR FORCE IN AREAS THE CONCENTRATION
RATIOS OF WHICH ARE UNDER 50 PER CENT[a]

Number of Firms	Type of Concentration Measure	
	Maximum	Overall
1	99.4	99.9
4	96.3	99.7
10	90.4	99.1

[a] Source: Table 5.

(1948) reports to the Bureau; it was these detailed and comprehensive tabulations of firms by employment size, industry, and county which made the study feasible. The denominators are interpolated estimates based on 1940 and 1950 Census data.

The fact that Overall concentration ratios tend to understate the level of concentration and that Maximum ratios tend to overstate it makes it possible to use cumulative relative frequency distributions of these sets of data to bracket the "true" level of concentration. Thus the first row of data in Table 30 may be interpreted in the following way: the percentage of areas studied in which the "true" concentration ratio of the largest firm is under 50 per cent is not less than 97.7 nor more than 99.7.

The percentages in Table 30 are impressively large. In order to see if these magnitudes would hold if the percentages referred to were of employed labor rather than areas, the cumulative relative frequency distributions were recomputed, counting each area not once but as many times as there are employees within it. Table 31 contains that portion of the resulting distribution that is comparable to that of Table 30.

These data may be interpreted in the same way as before: the top row shows that the proportion of employed labor force, in those areas in which the single largest firm employed less than 50 per cent of the total local labor force, was not less than 99.4 per cent nor more than 99.9 per cent of the aggregate employment of all 1,774 areas. Similar statements may be made for the four and ten largest firms. Whatever the qualifications and however awkward the statement, it is clear that the term "impressively large" is even more appropriate with respect to percentage-of-employees data than to percentage-of-areas data; clearly the relatively few areas that are high in concentration are smaller than average in the number of employed workers they contain.

What has been said thus far refers to the absolute level of concentration in local labor market areas. The remainder of the study concerns the following other characteristics of concentration: firm size, labor force size, industry, and geographic location. For purposes of these investigations it was considered desirable to look at all 1,774 areas and at those areas outstandingly high in concentration; where feasible this was done. There was some disagreement among the six measures as to which areas ranked highest in concentration. A summary index was used to arbitrate among the conflicting indications; this index was computed from the formula for the area under that portion of the concentration "curve" determined by the one-, four-, and ten-firm concentration ratios. This area was found twice—once using the three Overall ratios and once using the three Maximum ratios—for each of the top 150 labor markets; then, for each market, the simple mean of these two areas was obtained. The 100 labor markets ranking highest according to this mean were selected as the "top 100" markets.

The next problem investigated concerned the relative sizes of the largest firms in labor market areas, to see if any patterns of size relationships existed and if these patterns changed with concentration. The 1,774 areas were ranked by concentration and divided into ten concentration-rank classes. The following inequality ratios were computed for each of these classes:

$$E_1/E_{1\text{-}4} \quad , \quad E_1/E_{1\text{-}10} \quad , \quad E_{1\text{-}4}/E_{1\text{-}10}$$

where E_1 represents the sum of the employment of the (single) largest firms of all areas in the class; $E_{1\text{-}4}$ represents the

TABLE 32
INEQUALITY RATIOS FOR THE TOP AND BOTTOM CLASSES
OF AREAS AS RANKED BY CONCENTRATION[a]

Areas Ranking	Inequality Ratios		
	E_1/E_{1-4}	E_1/E_{1-10}	E_{1-4}/E_{1-10}
In top 10 per cent	.569	.482	.846
In bottom 10 per cent	.334	.188	.562

[a] Source: Table 12.

sum of the employment of all of the four top-ranking firms in each area within the class; and E_{1-10} represents the total employment of the ten top-ranking firms of all areas within the class. Table 32 shows these three inequality ratios for the highest- and lowest-ranking classes.

These data show the degree of firm inequality to be greater in high concentration areas than in low concentration areas; in fact, the change indicated by these extreme classes was found to be a smooth one, continuing almost without interruption or reversal throughout all ten concentration classes. As concentration increases the size of the largest firm increases both in comparison with the four largest firms and with the ten largest; similarly, the combined size of the four largest firms increases relative to that of the ten largest. Examination of the top 100 areas showed that the process of increasing inequality is accelerated among areas very high in concentration. Thus, the median values of these ratios for the twenty labor market areas which ranked highest according to the summary index measure were .746, .721, and .922. The data, therefore, leave little doubt that increasing concentration is a process accompanied by a tendency for one or a very few firms to occupy an especially dominant position in local labor markets.

The investigation of the absolute level of concentration provided as a by-product several indications that concentration and community size are inversely related. It was this relationship that was next examined. First, the 1,774 areas were ranked according to each of the six concentration measures and these rankings were broken into five classes, each containing 20 per cent of the areas. The employed labor force of each of the resulting thirty classes was found and ex-

TABLE 33

RELATIVE SIZE OF LABOR FORCE PER AREA AND CONCENTRATION
FOR TWO CLASSES OF AREAS[a]

Areas Ranking	Labor Force Relatives		
	Maximum-1	Maximum-4	Maximum-10
In top 20 per cent	43.0	48.0	51.5
In bottom 20 per cent	265.1	267.4	261.5

[a] Source: Table 13.

pressed as a ratio to the figure determined by taking one-fifth
of the total employed labor force of all 1,774 areas; the resulting figures, multiplied by 100, are relatives that make it possible to compare the mean size of the labor forces of areas in
each class with that of all areas. Table 33 shows the relatives
of six of these classes. The results are clear: the average size
of areas increases as concentration decreases.

The effort to bring out further aspects of this relationship, however, produced results considerably less impressive.
The 1,774 areas were ranked by labor force size and broken
into ten classes, each containing roughly 10 per cent of the
areas. Medians and means of all concentration measures
were found for each of these classes. The Overall-1 medians
are reproduced in Table 34, and except for the smallest and
largest classes, they obviously show little of the inverse correlation so strikingly in evidence in Table 33. The computation of a rank correlation coefficient, using a 105-area general

TABLE 34

MEDIAN CONCENTRATION RATIOS FOR TEN CLASSES OF AREAS
(OVERALL-1 RANKINGS)[a]

Labor Force Size	Median
0- 3,999	8
4,000- 5,499	5
5,500- 6,999	4
7,000- 8,499	4
8,500- 9,999	4
10,000-12,499	5
12,500-14,999	4
15,000-19,999	5
20,000-34,999	5
35,000 and Over	3

[a] Source: Table 14.

random sample, gave support to the interpretation suggested by Table 34: the coefficient between the rankings according to labor force size and Maximum-4 concentration ratios was minus .1678.

Further investigation of the discrepancy between the interpretations fostered by the data of Tables 33 and 34 involved a closer scrutiny of the very large, very small, and intermediate-sized areas. Each group was ranked by concentration and broken roughly into thirds; the mean labor force sizes of these subgroups were determined. The increases in these means as concentration decreased was orderly and smooth among the very large and very small areas, but it did not occur in the intermediate class. This and the fact that about 80 per cent of the areas were included in the intermediate class are the aspects of the data that are so clearly shown in Table 34. On the other hand, the large-area class contained just about two-thirds of the total employed labor force, and the inverse concentration-community-size relationship was very strong among these areas; it is these aspects of the data that dominate the view provided by Table 33.

The top 100 areas were also examined for evidence on the inverse relationship between community size and concentration. The evidence obtained suggested a stronger inverse correlation than did the all-areas evidence in that (a) there were no extremely large (in terms of labor force size) areas among the top 100, (b) the percentage of very small areas was larger among the top 100 areas than among all 1,774 areas, and (c) the rank correlation coefficient between concentration and size for the 100 areas was minus .3408.

The conclusion toward which these investigations lead is that, however measured, concentration and labor force size show an inverse relationship. High concentration is found among areas of all sizes, except for the very largest. In general, these very large areas are characterized by especially low concentration and the very small areas are characterized by especially high concentration. These are the sorts of results that a random distribution of firms among labor market areas would tend to provide. In fact, the hypothesis that this size-concentration relationship is the random result of the distribution of firms among labor market areas is so satisfactory that the major remaining issue, at this stage of the analysis, was why the lapse in this relationship occurred among the areas of intermediate size; the random hypothesis would not lead one to expect such a development. This suggests that the data contain other systematic elements.

The investigation of industry characteristics of concentration had several aspects. It was considered desirable, first of all, to see if the total industrial structure of concentrated areas differed from that of non-concentrated areas. This was accomplished by comparing a percentage distribution of the labor force by industry of the top 100 areas with a similar distribution for another 100 areas with comparable labor force sizes. The relationship of the two percentage distributions is shown in Table 35: the "industry relatives" were obtained by dividing the industry percentages of the 100 comparable areas into those of the 100 high concentration areas and multiplying the results by 100. The data clearly show high concentration areas to have distorted industrial structures, in that "mining" and "manufacturing" are both approximately twice as large as "normal." Further analysis revealed that the extent of mining distortion was inversely related to the labor force size of areas whereas that of manufacturing was directly related to labor force size.

Turning next to problems relating to the industrial characteristics of the large firms in the two groups of 100 areas, it was found that certain industries are disproportionately represented among the top-ranking firms of areas. For purposes of this investigation a finer classification system of industry

TABLE 35

PERCENTAGE DISTRIBUTION OF LABOR FORCE OF 100 HIGH CONCENTRATION AREAS BY INDUSTRY RELATIVE TO A COMPARABLE DISTRIBUTION FOR 100 NOT-HIGH CONCENTRATION AREAS[a]

Industry	Labor Force Relatives
Agriculture	57
Mining	187
Construction	71
Manufacturing	201
Transportation	75
Wholesale and retail trade	82
Finance, insurance, and real estate	75
Business and personal services	78
Professional and related services	89
All other	65

[a] Source: Table 18.

than that of Table 35 was used, and it showed the following industries to be those of greatest concentration: "mining," "textile mill products," "lumber and wood products," "paper and allied products," "chemicals and allied products," "primary metal industries," "machinery, except electrical," "electrical machinery," and "transportation equipment." These industries together accounted for 25.8 per cent of the United States total covered (by OASI) employment in 1948, 26.1 per cent of total covered employment in the 100 comparative areas, and 54.9 per cent of the total covered employment in the top 100 areas; but they accounted for 64.5 per cent of the employment of the single largest firms in the 100 comparative areas and 87.8 per cent of the employment of these firms in the 100 top concentration areas. There is no question but that (a) the employment of top-ranking firms in labor market areas is distributed more toward certain industries than toward others; (b) these high concentration industries are the ones listed above; and (c) the dominance of these industries among the firms that are relatively largest in their areas increases with concentration. Since, as mentioned above, the 100 areas used throughout the industry analysis had labor force size characteristics very much like those of the 100 high concentration areas, it is highly improbable that these conclusions are a reflection of the concentration-community-size relationship. Further support for the conclusion that industry is an independent factor is provided by the finding that only four of the nine industries ("mining," "textiles," "lumber," and "paper") were distributed disproportionately toward labor market areas that might be described as not-large labor market areas (areas other than standard metropolitan areas).

However, the employments of all nine of the industries definitely were distributed disproportionately toward large firms: the mean firm size in all industries covered by OASI was 13, whereas that of these nine industries varied from 19 to 271; the mean percentage of covered firms hiring 100 or more workers for all industries was 1.7, whereas the means of these industries varied from 3.4 to 28.8; and whereas these nine industries together accounted for only 4.8 per cent of the total number of covered firms, they accounted for 26.7 per cent of the firms hiring 100-499 workers and 44.0 per cent of the firms hiring 500 or more.

These industry findings do not rule out the possibility

opposite to that rejected two paragraphs above: namely, that the community-size-concentration relationship is but a reflection of the industry-concentration relationship. Further investigation suggested that this was not the case, but rather that these two variables exercised independent influences upon concentration. They clearly were related to each other, however, in the sense that certain industries ("mining," "lumber," "paper," and "chemicals") were more prominent among small labor market areas, others ("machinery, except electrical," "electrical machinery," and "transportation equipment") were more important in larger areas, and still others ("textiles" and "primary metal industries") appeared to exert an impact upon both small and large labor markets.

Both the top 100 areas data and all 1,774 areas data showed strong regional characteristics. The analytical question which this raised was: To what extent can regional variations in concentration be "explained" by the two factors already shown to be related to concentration, community size, and industry? The attempt to answer this question consisted of a multiple correlation analysis of three sets of regional measures. The "dependent" measures (of concentration) were percentages of the regional labor forces found in the top-ranking 90 per cent of all 1,774 areas. The "independent" measures of regional "community size" were percentages of regional labor forces found in the smallest (as measured by size of labor force) 70 per cent of all 1,774 areas. And the measures of the other "independent" variable, "industry," were relatives that roughly indicated the disproportionate distribution of the nine high concentration industries toward the not-large areas of the regions. The multiple correlation coefficient computed with these measures was plus .89; this coefficient is high enough to be consistent with the hypothesis that regional concentration characteristics are largely explainable in terms of labor force size and the distribution of industry.

This conclusion was buttressed by a series of "experiments" in which the data, from which were derived the regional measures used in the correlation computation, were examined for the possibility of their containing systematic variation other than that attributed to the influence of industry and community size. For example, two regions with roughly equal community size characteristics would be investigated to see if the variation in their concentration measures corresponded with that of their industry measures. The consistency with which this sort of correspondence occurred suggested that these experiments took into account all of the sources of systematic regional variation in concentration.

One set of these experiments involved "holding concentration constant" (choosing two regions with roughly equal concentration measures) and investigating the relationship between the other two measures, community size and industry. Consistently they were inversely related: that is, one region would be "high" according to one measure and the other region would be "high" according to the other measure. The simple correlation coefficient between the two sets of nine measures was minus .67—the nine high concentration industries tended to be located predominately in regions with the smallest portions of their labor forces located in relatively small labor market areas. This "conflict" between the forces that produce concentration undoubtedly is the main factor that explains why the concentration-community-size relationship appeared to be weaker than suggested by the random hypothesis. If the data had been standardized for industry, the increase in community size as concentration decreased would have been much more obvious. Support for this conclusion was provided by a partial coefficient of correlation (computed in connection with the multiple coefficient referred to above) between community size and concentration of plus .89. This coefficient means that there is a very strong tendency for concentration to be greatest in those regions which have the largest percentages of their labor forces distributed toward "smaller" labor market areas, industry being "held constant."

The body of concentration ratios from which the "findings" summarized above were obtained are not without serious shortcomings. It was impossible to do anything about most of them, so the problem of estimating the extent of error remaining in the data presented itself.

One of the most unfortunate aspects of the data lay in the fact that the BOASI sources from which individual firm employment figures were obtained did not show the distribution of firm employment by skill category. As pointed out earlier in this summary, this made it necessary to limit the study to the not-skilled portion of the labor force and to adopt a bracketing technique—with Overall ratios being less than and Maximum ratios being greater than the "true" concentration ratios—for estimating the three points on the concentration curves of the labor markets studied. This was the reason for presenting the absolute level of concentration in a not-less-than-nor-greater-than fashion.

The other major data difficulty lay in the fact that certain types of firms were not subject to coverage under the OASI program in 1948: those excluded "firms" large enough to be troublesome were railroads, non-profit firms (chiefly hospitals and educational institutions), and "government." The technique used to estimate the error resulting from these exclusions was crude indeed: for each labor market area, the total number of workers in each of the relevant census categories was estimated for 1948 from 1950 Census data and was considered to be employed by a single firm; these "firm" figures were used in a recomputation of the concentration ratios for each of two samples—a random one and one drawn from among the high concentration areas. These sample ratios were first adjusted for the presence of railroad firms alone, since there is a question as to the appropriateness of including government and non-profit "firms" in a study oriented toward monopsony. The results were that concentration rose by an average amount as high as 12.73 per cent for one (Maximum-4) of the six measures in the random sample and for an average as high as 3.59 per cent for two (Overall-10 and Maximum-10) of the measures in the high concentration sample areas. Next, the same two samples were adjusted for the presence of railroads, non-profit firms, and government "firms" simultaneously; the resulting average percentage increases were large, as great as 75.50 per cent among the random sample areas and 18.48 per cent among the areas of the high concentration sample.

There were several data difficulties in addition to the two mentioned above, but only four of them involved error of serious magnitude. The first of these may be called "the transitory problem." It grew out of the fact that the firm employment data, from which the numerators of the concentration ratios were obtained, refer to mid-March 1948; because of this the data contain elements of a purely transitory nature, whereas they should reflect only the "stabilized" or "permanent" employment of the large firms. It was impossible to adjust the data by removing cyclical, random, trend, and seasonal elements. However, it was possible to compute an "outside" estimate of the magnitude of the error resulting from the presence of these elements over a one-year period; they appeared to be such as to make the ratios 9 per cent too large for a randomly chosen sample of areas and 14 per cent too large for a sample of high concentration areas.

Another data difficulty grew out of the uncertainty as to whether the "reporting units" (the term used to refer to covered business units in BOASI literature) were firms or establishments; there were special circumstances under which they could be either. It was possible to run a check on the extent of the possible error involved in a small random sample of areas, and concentration ratios were recomputed from reporting unit data that had been adjusted in such a way as to be uniformly on a firm basis. The resulting percentage increase in concentration ratios was estimated to be no greater than 5 per cent, on the average.

Another source of ambiguity concerning the concentration ratios presented in this study was discovered when employment ratios were compared with payroll ratios. The BOASI data sources provided covered employment and payrolls for individual firms and for whole counties, so that it was possible to compute comparable ratios using exclusively employment or exclusively payroll data. This was done for several samples of data with highly variable results; the payroll ratios exceeded employment ratios by amounts averaging from 12 to 27 per cent. An attempt to evaluate the reality and significance of these differences proved largely abortive. A portion of the differences was found to be "unreal" in that it probably arose from the exclusion of self-employed workers from the data, and the evaluation of the remaining differences involved a decision as to whether those differences represented firm efforts to compensate for disadvantages of size or to hire "a better quality" of labor. Neither of these aspects of the discrepancy between the two types of ratios was investigated extensively, so its significance for the reliability of the ratios presented here remains uncertain.

Finally, there was a reassessment of the procedure used in computing Maximum concentration ratios. That procedure, it will be recalled, involved deducting certain groups of workers from the denominators of Overall ratios. One of the deleted groups was unskilled farm labor; this deletion was made in deference to the widely held belief that this portion of the not-skilled labor market is significantly insulated from the rest of that market in the short run. This view may not be correct. Investigation showed that the reinsertion of these employees in the denominators of Maximum concentration ratios caused them to decline by average amounts of 7 per cent and 11 per cent, for random and high concentration areas respectively.

The desirability of the railroad, transitory, firm-establishment, and agricultural adjustments appears to be reasonably evident. If their magnitudes are approximated by the estimates that have been outlined above, it appears likely that the concentration position of the high concentration areas has been overstated between 5 and 20 per cent, whereas that of most other areas may have been understated by an amount not greater than 9 per cent. If future research should indicate that it is appropriate to include government and non-profit "firms" on a completely parallel basis with private, profit-oriented "firms" in a study of this sort, crude estimates suggest that the general level of concentration may be substantially raised—so that the aggregate upward adjustment may go as high as 72 per cent. However, even the extreme adjustment procedures adopted for purposes of this estimate did not drastically raise the estimated concentration of the areas already high in concentration; the net effect of all adjustments on these areas varied from minus 20 per cent for the Maximum-1 measures to plus 10 per cent for the Overall-10 measures.

The major finding of this study is that the extent of concentration among private, profit-oriented firms in the not-skilled portions of local labor markets is low. Even if it should turn out that the error in the estimates presented here were such that *all* ratios should be *doubled*, the number of workers in labor markets, the four largest firms of which hire less than 50 per cent of the employed labor force, would still be quite large: roughly, between 78 and 94 per cent of the employed labor force. Such low concentration appears to be consistent with an explanation that runs largely in terms of chance; that is, it seems probable that at least the observed degree of concentration would exist if the opportunity for monopsony gains in labor markets were not a factor in plant location decision-making. This point may be made, perhaps more controversially, in another way. There are a great many labor market areas in which the degree of concentration is quite low; most of these are small enough to give large firms (singly, or in two's and three's) a wide variety of locations within which they might achieve highly dominant positions in the market for not-skilled labor—and, perhaps, even more dominant positions in regard to the skilled component of their work forces. To the extent that the monopsony gains to be obtained in labor markets are real and quantitatively significant, this appears to mean that American businessmen are grossly neglecting opportunities for decreasing their outlays on this most important factor of production. The scale of this neglect demands explanation. It may not be inconsistent with the belief that monopsony theory has an important role to play in explaining wage rate determination in the United States, but the need for reconciliation should be evident.

EPILOGUE

I have emphasized throughout that this is a study of concentration and that testing the monopsony-concentration hypothesis is beyond its scope. However, the process of revising it for publication was a long and not very exciting one. Primarily as a diversion from this chore, I began to think of ways to conduct a test. It soon became clear that there were data immediately at hand which could be used for this purpose. The urge to begin examining the hypothesis with these data proved to be irresistible, and so a series of experiments was initiated. The results of these experiments suggest little or no relationship between concentration and wages. Having said this, I must hasten to add that the analysis was by no means a definitive one; rather, it is presented as an exploratory first step that was quite arbitrarily discontinued when the revision of the main body of the study was completed. The details of this investigation are presented in Section 16 of the Appendix.

DATA SOURCES, PROCEDURES, ESTIMATES OF
ERROR, AND OTHER SUPPLEMENTARY
DETAILS

The sources of data from which the concentration ratios
of this study were computed, the procedures involved, and
certain shortcomings of these data and procedures have been
indicated in various degrees of detail at several points in the
text. This appendix has several purposes: first, certain minor
data difficulties, not previously considered, will be introduced
and, where possible, appraised as sources of error in the concentration ratios; second, more detail will be provided about
those more important difficulties presented and described in
Chapter II; third, certain supplementary operations performed in connection with Chapter III will be described in
more detail; finally, a brief excursion into a test of the concentration-monopsony hypothesis will be described. Generally speaking, this appendix will be of no interest to many
readers. It is designed to facilitate further work in this area
of economic analysis. Specifically, the details presented here
may make it possible for others to avoid certain problems that
caused much fumbling in this initial effort; they may permit
others to retrace steps taken here or to produce similar data
with a minimum of difficulty; or they may provide information needed for establishing the comparability of related concentration measures.

1. DATA SOURCES AND PROCEDURES

Two sets of three concentration ratios—six ratios in all—
were computed for each of the 1,774 labor market areas included in this study. The first set, referred to as Overall
ratios, have as their numerators the employment of the largest, the four largest, and the ten largest firms and, as their

denominators, a census-derived estimate of the 1948 total employment of all firms. These ratios are handled throughout the study as percentages—thus, for each labor market, they represent the percentages of the total employed labor force of that market hired by these three groupings of the largest firms in that market. The other set of three ratios, called Maximum ratios, have the same three numerators but a different denominator; this denominator is a census-derived estimate of the not-skilled component of the total employed labor force. The two sets of ratios may be thought of as pairs of estimates of the percentage of not-skilled workers hired by three different groupings of the largest firms in each labor market, the pairs probably bracketing the "true" ratios of these groupings of large firms.

In addition to these six ratios—from which all of the major findings of Chapter III are drawn—three other special-purpose types of ratios were devised. The first of these consisted of ratios that had the same numerators as the Overall and Maximum ratios but which used BOASI "covered employment" as denominators; the second consisted of ratios that had January-March, 1948, payroll (rather than employment) figures in numerators and denominators. These two sets of ratios were found to be useful in certain of the investigations of Chapter II and this appendix. The other special-purpose ratios were Overall-30 and Maximum-30, designed to provide information about concentration as it appears when a "very large" number of firms is considered. All of these ratios were described adequately in the text.

The date of the study was determined by the availability of the BOASI employer data. The sources of these data were two IBM tabulations, based upon 1948 first-quarter reports of business establishments covered by Old-Age and Survivors Insurance as of that date and the *County Business Patterns* series of publications. One of the tabulations, the Time-Series, presented the employment of covered firms hiring 100 or more workers by state, county, and industry for the first quarters of 1947 and 1948. This tabulation was one of the "first runs" of the 1948 data used by the Employers Section, Statistics Branch, Bureau of Old-Age and Survivors Insurance, to check for errors. It was designed so that rapid comparisons between 1947 and 1948 data could be made on an individual firm basis; where changes in location or unreasonable changes in employment or wage information appeared, reference was made to more basic sources to see if the changes were real or were only the result of error in reporting or processing. Since it included all reporting units hiring 100 or more workers (during the pay period ending nearest March 15, 1948), this tabulation, supplemented by a delinquent reports tabulation, was the only source of firm data used for those labor market areas that contained as many as ten firms in the 100-and-over employee-size category. For those areas that had less than ten firms of this size, recourse to the other tabulation, Table 615, was necessitated, for this tabulation contained employment data for firms of all sizes. It differed from the Time-Series in that firms were not listed separately or identified by code numbers. Thus if there were three firms in an industry subgroup in a given firm-size category, the employment of these three would be presented as a single figure; allocating the total employment among the three firms was done in such a way as to overstate concentration. This tabulation represented the final form of the data; the *County Business Patterns* bulletins were prepared from it. The bulletins provide (for state, county, and industry) mid-March 1948 employment, taxable payrolls (January to March, 1948), and the number of firms by the following employment-size categories: 0-3, 4-7, 8-19, 20-49, 50-99, 100-499, 500 or more.[1]

Obtaining the numerators was a three-step process. First it was necessary to determine which labor market areas would be studied. The criterion used was that the selected areas must contain at least one firm hiring 100 or more workers, so this step was accomplished rapidly by reference to the employee-size frequency distributions in the bulletins. Next, employment figures for firms hiring 100 or more employees were obtained from the Time-Series. If there were less than ten firms hiring this many workers, the third and last step consisted of obtaining employment figures on the remaining firms from Table 615.

1. The Time-Series is labeled "Job 8055, Operation 103, 1947 vs. 1948: Comparison of 100 and Over Listings." Table 615 is labeled "Job 8055, Part XIII. First Quarter 1948 Employer Data: Combined Single and Multi-Unit Employers. Table 615." Both of these tabulations are located in the Employer Section, Statistics Branch, of the Bureau of Old-Age and Survivors Insurance. Footnote 10, Chapter I provides complete reference information for *County Business Patterns*.

The procedure for allocating the combined employment figures of Table 615 among firms is described in Section 2 of this appendix.

The denominators used for computing the two major sets of concentration ratios are based on census data. The first of these is an estimate of the total number of employed workers in the areas in 1948. For each area, this denominator was determined by assuming that the civilian labor force changed in a straight-line fashion between 1940 and 1950;[2] the 1948 labor force was decreased by a percentage figure that represented the level of unemployment at that time.[3] Specifically, the procedure for each area was as follows: the 1950 civilian labor force was obtained from the 1950 Census.[4] From this was deducted the 1940 civilian labor force. This difference was multiplied by two-tenths and the resulting figure was deducted from the 1950 civilian labor force—except for those areas whose labor forces decreased over the ten-year interval, and in these cases the figure obtained by multiplying the difference by two-tenths was *added* to the 1950 civilian labor force. The resulting estimate of the 1948 labor force was multiplied by 96.4 per cent, the estimated nation-wide level of employment at that time,[5] to obtain the estimated employed civilian labor force. This denominator was used to obtain Overall concentration ratios.

A slight complication in the above procedures grew out of the fact that the 1940 Census did not provide a figure comparable with the "civilian labor force" of the 1950 Census. At the suggestion of Howard G. Brunsman of the Bureau of the Census,[6] the following procedure was adopted: the 1940 estimated civilian population of counties as presented in a special population report[7] was deducted from the 1940 Census total population for each area; the resulting difference was deducted from the "in labor force" figure presented in the 1940 Census.[8]

The denominator for Maximum concentration ratios repre-

2. See Section 7, this appendix.
3. See Section 7, this appendix.
4. U.S. Bureau of the Census, *1950 Census of Population. General Characteristics.* Series P-B preprints of Volume II, Table 43.
5. U.S. Bureau of Labor Statistics, *Monthly Labor Review*, LXVII (1948), 72.
6. This suggestion was made in a letter to the author of this study, dated December 5, 1952.
7. U.S. Bureau of the Census, *Estimated Civilian Population of the United States, by Counties: November 1, 1943.* Special Reports of the Population, Series P-44, No. 3.
8. U.S. Bureau of the Census, *County Data Book: A Supplement to the Statistical Abstract of the United States* (Washington: Government Printing Office, 1947), Table 3.

sents an estimate of what has been referred to in the body of this study as the "not-skilled" employed labor force. It was obtained by computing for each area a ratio of the 1950 not-skilled employed to the 1950 total employed labor force; the Overall denominator was then multiplied by this ratio and the result was the desired estimate. The procedure for obtaining the not-skilled ratio is described in footnote 3, Chapter II.

2. Table 615 Estimating Procedure and Error

Whereas the employment of each firm is given individually in the Time-Series tabulation, the employment of several firms is often combined in Table 615. This occurs any time two or more firms are in the same firm-size and industry classification. The estimating procedure used to isolate the employment of these combined firms lends a conservative bias to the data—it causes concentration to be overstated. The purpose of this section is to describe the procedure used and to provide an estimate of the degree of misrepresentation of concentration which it involves.

To illustrate the nature of this problem consider a hypothetical county in which there were seven firms hiring 100 or more employees in 1948; these firm figures would be obtained from the Time-Series, where they are presented individually. Assume further that the appropriate *County Business Patterns* bulletin indicates that there were five firms in the 50-99 employee-size category. Since the Time-Series contains no data on firms hiring less than 100 employees, it would be necessary to refer to Table 615 for the employee-size of these firms. Suppose Table 615 showed that all of them were in "manufacturing": one, in "food and kindred products," hired seventy-five workers; one, in "tobacco manufactures," hired eighty workers; and three, in "rubber products," hired a total of 204 workers. The employment of the last three firms would be combined since all of them were in the same industry subclassification and firm-size category. The estimating procedure to be used here would involve allocating these workers in such a way as to maximize concentration within the limits permitted by the form in which the data are presented. In this particular hypothetical example, the allocation rule would dictate the assignment of ninety-nine workers to one firm, fifty to another, and fifty-five to the third.

In the above hypothetical case the seven largest firms' employments would be those obtained from the Time-Series, that of the eighth-ranking firm would be the estimated ninety-nine, and those of the ninth and tenth firms would be eighty and seventy-five respectively. Because of the use of the estimated figure, ninety-nine, the concentration ratio of the *ten largest firms* would probably be too large. In this case the concentration ratio for the *four largest firms* would not be affected, although it probably would have been had there been less than four firms in the 100-and-over size class. Since this labor market area would not have qualified for consideration in the study unless it contained at least one firm with 100 or more employees, the concentration ratio determined by using the *single largest firm* could not have been affected by this estimating procedure in any area.[9]

Since this procedure was necessitated in the majority of areas which had less than ten firms in the 100-or-more category, the problem of estimating its effect upon the concentration ratios presents itself.

Referring again to the hypothetical county discussed above, a means of estimating the range of error in the ten-largest numerator may be found by reallocating the total employment of the (three) combined firms in such a way as to *minimize* their contribution to concentration—by assuming each to have had 204/3 or 68 employees. Under this assumption the eighth-largest and ninth-largest firms would hire 80 and 75 employees respectively, and the tenth-largest firm would be assigned an employment figure of 68—thus providing a new total employment figure for the ten top-ranking firms which is less than the previous total by 31 (99 minus 68) workers. Concentration ratios determined through the use of these two types of numerators provide the upper and lower limits within which the actual concentration ratio must lie.

In order to estimate the magnitude of this error, a sample of forty areas[10] was investigated. In eleven of the sample areas, there were ten or more firms hiring 100 or more workers; in these areas all data were obtained from the Time-Series, where all firm data are provided separately, so the

9. A small portion of the Time-Series was lost and this made it necessary to get the single-largest firm figures for a few areas from Table 615; thus the statement in the text is not completely correct. See Section 4 in this appendix.

10. These areas constituted a random subsample drawn from the 105-area general random sample described in footnote 31 below.

problem under consideration did not arise. In twenty of the forty areas there were less than four firms hiring 100 or more workers, and in the other nine areas there were at least four but not more than nine firms hiring 100 or more workers; hence the possibility of estimating error arose in the determination of twenty Overall-4 and Maximum-4 concentration ratios and in twenty-nine Overall-10 and Maximum-10 concentration ratios. Numerators of these areas were redetermined in the minimum concentration fashion and all concentration ratios were recomputed. The average range between lower and upper limits of the whole forty-area sample was found to be as follows: Overall-4, 0.05 of one percentage point; Maximum-4, 0.14 of one percentage point; Overall-10, 0.23 of one percentage point; and Maximum-10, 0.61 of one percentage point. Since in no case did the estimating procedure used with Table 615 bring about as much as a single point of overstatement in concentration percentages, it is clear that this overstatement is small enough that its effect upon the absolute levels of concentration and upon the relative rankings of areas within the distributions may safely be neglected.

3. Errors in the Time-Series Data

As pointed out in Section 1 of this appendix, the Time-Series was one of the first "runs" of the first quarter, 1948, data made by the BOASI; its purpose was to permit a check on the large-firms data. There were errors in these data— firms were mislocated, their employments were misstated, etc.—which BOASI investigators discovered by means of this tabulation; many of these were indicated in pencil on the tabulation itself. However, there were other errors in the tabulation which had not been discovered or, if discovered, had not been noted. Some of these were disclosed by the process used in extracting data for purposes of this study. Others were simply omissions that were provided by a supplementary "delinquent reports" tabulation. The aim of this section is that of estimating the magnitude of the inaccuracies in the concentration ratios deriving from errors in the Time-Series data which were not noted on the tabulation, not corrected by the use of the delinquent reports tabulation, or not "discovered" in the extractive process.

Table 615 presents the first quarter, 1948, data after all corrections have been made; it was from this tabulation that

the data in the *County Business Patterns* bulletins were derived. The process by which these accurate data sources were
used to check and supplement the less accurate Time-Series
data can best be indicated by hypothetical illustrations.

Assume that a bulletin showed County "A" to include no
firms in the over-500 (employee firm-size) category and thirteen firms in the 100-499 category; but the Time-Series presented only twelve firms in the 100-499 category. Reference
would be made to Table 615 from which the employment of
the missing firm would be gotten.

Assume that the appropriate state bulletin showed County
"B" to include seven firms hiring 500 or more workers, and
ten firms in the 100-499 size category; the Time-Series provided data for seventeen firms, seven of which actually had
500 or more employees. The seventeen firms would be assumed to be correct; no reference to Table 615 would be made.

Assume that the bulletin showed eight firms in the 100-499
category, and none in the 500-and-over category; but the Time-
Series presented nine firms in the 100-499 category. Table
615 would be consulted to determine which of the nine firms
did not belong in County "C."

Counties such as the hypothetical ones above are labeled
"complete-check" counties. By this is meant that a complete
check has been made on all firms *in the 100-and-over categories* and that all discrepancies between the bulletins and
Time-Series have been reconciled by pencil corrections in the
Time-Series, by the delinquent reports supplement, or by
reference to Table 615. In all such counties, then, the data on
100-and-over firms are assumed to be accurate.

In some counties it was impractical to check the accuracy
of Time-Series data of all firms hiring 100 or more workers.
To illustrate, assume that the appropriate bulletin showed
County "D" to contain seven firms in the 500-and-over size
category and fifty-five firms in the 100-499 class. In such a
case, if more or less than seven of the large-category firms
were shown in the Time-Series (as corrected or as supplemented by the delinquent reports tabulation) reference would
be made to Table 615 and the employment of these seven firms
determined accurately. A *complete* check of the data in
County "D" would require that the firms in the 100-499 size
class listed in the Time-Series be counted; if this count revealed more or less than fifty-five firms, the discrepancy would

have to be eliminated by reference to Table 615; at that point, then, the three largest of the fifty-five firms could be used with the other seven (500-and-over) firms as the firm employment figures for County "D." In situations comparable with this one, the time-cost of checking the large number of Time-Series firms in the 100-499 class against those in Table 615 was prohibitive. Consequently, the three largest Time-Series firms in the 100-499 size classification were accepted without the Table 615 cross-check. Counties such as "D" are labeled "partial-check" areas. In them there is some positive number less than ten, of firms in the 500-and-over category, the discrepancies of which have been checked against Table 615—so these data are assumed to be accurate—and the remainder of the ten largest firms are 100-499 sized firms which have not been checked for discrepancies.

Finally, there were counties in which the cost of checking any of the Time-Series data against the more accurate tabulation was prohibitive. To cite an extreme case, there were 2,050 firms in the 100-499 size classification and 388 firms in the 500-and-over category in Cook County, Illinois. In such a county, the ten largest firms in the Time-Series were accepted, and no attempt was made to check the accuracy of these employment figures by reference to Table 615.

The general rule-of-thumb with respect to these cross-checks on the Time-Series data was that no checks would be made for those counties for which the total number of firms to be checked exceeded twenty. Thus the counties included in this study may be put into three categories, as follows:

1. "Complete-check" counties were those in which: (a) the number of firms in the 500-and-over category was not less than ten nor more than twenty; or (b) the number of firms in the 500-and-over class was some positive number less than ten, and the number in the 100-499 category was such that the sum of it and those in the 500-and-over category did not exceed twenty; or (c) there were no firms in the 500-and-over class and those in the 100-499 category numbered not more than twenty.

2. "Partial-check" counties were those in which the number of firms in the 500-and-over class was a positive number less than ten, and the number of firms in the 100-499 class was such that the sum of it and the number in the 500-and-over category exceeded twenty.

3. ''No-check'' counties were those in which: (a) the number of firms in the 500-and-over category exceeded twenty; or (b) there were no firms in the 500-and-over category and the number in the 100-499 category was greater than twenty.

There were 1,706 complete-check counties, 169 partial-check counties, and 62 no-check counties.[11] Thus there were 62 areas in which no cross-check was run on the firms hiring 100 or more workers and 169 areas in which a cross-check was run only on a portion of those firms. It is impossible to estimate accurately the number of errors remaining in the firm employment figures for these areas. However, the number of errors found in the other areas suggests that the undiscovered error is not significantly large. The total number of Time-Series errors found in the complete-check areas and the checked portions of the partial-check areas numbered 234. Of these errors, 160 were corrected by pencil notations in the Time-Series or by the delinquent reports supplement; that is, 68 per cent of the total number of discrepancies discovered were corrected by these two means. In the no-check areas, these same two means produced eleven corrections to the Time-Series data. If the ratio of corrections by these means to total discrepancies was the same in those areas in which checks were unfeasible as it was in the checked areas, the total number of discrepancies in the unchecked portion was sixteen; assuming this to be accurate, five errors remain in the data after the eleven corrections.

There is another way to estimate the extent of uncorrected error. Assume that approximately one-half (84) of the partial-check counties are complete-check counties and the other one-half (85) are no-check counties. Now there are 1,790 complete-check counties and 147 no-check areas. There is a total of 234 discrepancies in the 1,790 complete-check areas— about 13 discrepancies per 100 areas. If the number of discrepancies per 100 areas were the same in the no-check counties, the total number of discrepancies would be approximately 19[12]—leaving 8 errors after the 11 corrections.

11. The figures in this sentence relate to counties before any combinations of them into metropolitan or non-metropolitan labor market areas were made. This accounts for the fact that the sum of the three figures is considerably greater than 1,774, which is the total number of labor market areas actually used in the study.

12. Actually, the ratio of errors per 100 counties should be larger in the no-check counties, since many of the complete-check counties contain only one or a

The above estimates are little more than crude guesses as to the number of firms included or excluded because of Time-Series inaccuracy. Nonetheless, the fact that both estimates are less than ten supports the conclusion that the undiscovered Time-Series error is very small.

4. LOST TABULATIONS

One of the shortcomings of the Time-Series as a source of data was the fact that part of the tabulation had been misplaced before this research project was initiated. The losses were not serious: data for all of Maine and two counties in New Hampshire were missing. This meant using Table 615 to obtain all firm data in these areas—the employment of firms hiring 100 or more employees as well as those hiring less than 100 had to be gotten from Table 615 in these counties. This was a less satisfactory procedure because the Time-Series provides individual firm-employment figures, whereas the employment of two or more firms might be presented compositely in Table 615, if those firms happened to be in the same industry and firm-size categories. Hence, estimating procedures—never necessary when data were obtained from the Time-Series—were frequently required when the data were extracted from Table 615.

Only seventeen areas (less than 1 per cent of the total studied) were involved, so the losses obviously could not be a terribly serious problem, even if the estimating procedures were poor. Within these areas the employments of eighty-two firms in the 100-and-over category were estimated and incorporated into concentration ratio computations. The estimating procedures used were such as to make concentration as high as possible given the uncertainties of the data. In order to provide an estimate of the extent to which this might tend to distort the concentration findings upward, the Maximum-1, Maximum-4, Maximum-10, and the Maximum-30 concentration ratios of the seventeen areas were recomputed in such a way as to *minimize* the concentration situation within the limits of the data ambiguities.[13] The seventeen overstated and understated concentration ratios differed by an average amount of 1.25 percentage points in Maximum-1, 2.03 per-

few firms hiring 100 or more workers, whereas all of the no-check counties contain more than ten such firms.

13. This procedure was discussed in Section 2 above.

centage points in Maximum-4, 1.74 percentage points in Maximum-10, and 4.40 percentage points in Maximum-30. This means that the real-world Maximum-1 concentration percentages of the seventeen areas cannot be less than those used herein (as far as the error due to the problem being discussed is concerned) by an amount in excess of 1.25 percentage points on the average, that the real-world Maximum-4 concentration percentages of the seventeen areas cannot be less than those used herein by an amount in excess of 2.03 percentage points on the average, etc. Given the small number of areas involved and the small ranges of error, it is clear that this estimating procedure could not have had an appreciable effect upon the total distribution of the 1,774 areas by any of the concentration measures. This, in turn, must mean that the absolute level findings are insignificantly affected by the process of estimating the employment of the large firms in the seventeen areas.

One of the seventeen was among the "top 100" areas which were given special attention in connection with the investigation of the absolute level and other characteristics of concentration. This labor market area achieved its high concentration position on the basis of overstated concentration ratios, as discussed above, so this raises a question as to whether the area really belongs there. To find the answer, the summary index for this area was recomputed using the *understated* set of ratios. The resulting summary index was high enough to place the area well above the least concentrated of the top 100 areas, so there is no question but that it would have been among the high concentration areas if actual rather than estimated firm employment figures had been available.

In addition to the Time-Series losses, one small section of Table 615 was missing; it included five counties in Minnesota. One of these contained no firms hiring more than 100 workers, so this county would not have been included in the study even if the Table 615 data had been available. Another county contained ten firms hiring more than 100 workers, so all the firm-employment figures were available in the Time-Series. The other three counties contained seven, one, and one firms with more than 100 workers. The Minnesota *County Business Patterns* bulletin showed the county with seven firms in the 100-499 employee size-category to have four firms in the 50-99 category; thus, for purposes of figuring concentration ratios, the eighth-, ninth-, and tenth-ranking firms of this area were all assumed to have the maximum possible number of employees—ninety-nine. One of the areas which contained only one firm with 100 or more workers was shown to contain no firms in the 50-99 firm-size category but twelve firms in the 20-49 category; thus concentration ratios for this area were computed on the assumption that the firms ranking two through ten all had forty-nine employees. The other area with only one firm in the 100-and-over category contained none in the 50-99 size category and only 8 in the 20-49 firm-size category. Thus it was assumed that firms ranking 2 through 9 had 49 employees and that the tenth-ranking firm had 19 employees; concentration ratios were computed accordingly. These procedures provided concentration ratios for the three areas which were surely too large: even so, all of them were relatively low—both Overall-10 and Maximum-10 ratios of the three areas were below the respective medians of the frequency distributions of all 1,774 areas according to these two concentration measures.

5. The "State-Wide" Problem

One of the deficiencies of the Bureau of Old-Age and Survivors Insurance data lay in the fact that there were a number of firms which were located by state but not by county within state. These were included in a catch-all category for each state called "state-wide"; they were not included in any of the computations of concentration ratios. Of all firms hiring 3.7 per cent of all covered employees, 1.6 per cent were so classified.[14] It is possible that the actual error in the concentration data might be greater than that suggested by the figure 1.6 per cent, since the percentage of all firms hiring 100 or more workers in the state-wide category was 4.8—i.e., "state-wide" firms were distributed disproportionately toward large firm-size categories.

Two excerpts from the explanatory comments in *County Business Patterns* are relevant to an appraisal of the extent of error brought about by not including state-wide firms in the computation of concentration ratios.

In some cases, however, a reporting unit may consist of several establishments, where a single employer operates two or more estab-

14. U.S. Department of Commerce, *1948 County Business Patterns*, Part 1, p. 5.

lishments of the same business activity in a single county or State. This rarely occurs in the manufacturing industries, but sometimes occurs in retail trade, construction, and service industries where a firm may operate many small branches or stores. Such establishments may then be grouped into county-wide or State-wide reporting units.[15]

Units unclassified by county are designated in the tables as "State-wide." This classification includes reporting units without a fixed location within the State, or with employees in more than one county, or of unknown county location.[16]

Clearly the writer of these explanatory notes would not have thought the omission of state-wide firms (reporting units) a serious source of error for purposes of computing concentration ratios. In addition, this problem was discussed by the author of this study with the people in the BOASI from whom the basic tabulations were obtained. They were of the opinion that state-wide firms were primarily multi-establishment firms which reported to the bureau through one central state office—"like A & P," as one of them expressed it.

The state-wide data themselves support this notion—and thus indirectly suggest that the firms involved do not seriously impair the accuracy of the concentration ratios. In the first place, the mean employment of all firms in the state-wide category is over twice that of all firms covered by OASI—30.8 as compared with 13.3. The likely explanation of this difference is that the state-wide "reporting units" are multi-establishment firms. In the second place, whereas the three industry categories, construction, wholesale trade, and retail trade, contribute only 22.7 per cent of the nation-wide total of firms in the 100-and-over employment size class, they contribute 58.9 per cent of the national total of *state-wide* 100-and-over sized firms.

It may be that there are firms in the state-wide category which are single-establishment firms and which, if properly relocated, would be among the top ten firms in their labor market areas—thus making recomputation of some of the concentration ratios in those areas necessary. Such evidence as there is, however, indicates that this would be an infrequent occurrence, not appreciably altering the basic data of the study.

15. *Ibid.*
16. *Ibid.*, p. 6.

6. Delinquent Firms

The Bureau of Old-Age and Survivors Insurance data are based on employers' tax reports for the first quarter of 1948. Some employers were late in submitting their reports. The tabulations used in this study included adjustments for only those delinquent reports received by the end of April, 1949.

The problem that arises in connection with these delinquents is essentially the same as that posed by the state-wide firms discussed in the preceding section of this appendix. And, unfortunately, the data are more fragmentary; inherently it is difficult to provide specifics about, for example, the industry or location of delinquent firms. With respect to the magnitude of this problem, the introductory explanatory notes in the *County Business Patterns* have this to say: "It is estimated that for the United States as a whole, reports received after the closing of these tabulations will account for about 2.6 per cent of the total number of reporting units, 0.6 per cent of March 1948 employment, and 0.4 per cent of total taxable pay rolls."[17]   These figures make it clear that the covered employment involved here is distributed disproportionately toward small firms.   The estimated mean employment of the delinquent firms is 3.1 whereas that of all firms covered by OASI in 1948 is 13.3.

The conclusion toward which these data lead—slightly less conclusively, perhaps—is similar to that of the preceding section.   There may be some delinquent firms which, if accounted for, would bring about some increase in some concentration ratios, but there would probably be few such cases— hence, this is unlikely to be a significant source of error in the concentration ratios presented and analyzed in this study.

7. Two Minor Sources of Error in the Denominators of Concentration Ratios

The process by which the denominators of Overall concentration ratios were computed may briefly be described as follows: the civilian labor force for each area for 1950 and for 1940 were obtained from census sources; the latter was deducted from the former; the difference was multiplied by 20 per cent; this product was deducted from, or added to, the 1950 civilian labor force depending on whether the 1950 figure

17. *Ibid.*, p. 5.

was, respectively, greater than or less than the 1940 figure. These steps provided a "straight line" estimate of the 1948 civilian labor force. Then this estimate was multiplied by 96.4 per cent, the estimated national percentage level of employment for March, 1948. The purpose of this section is that of commenting on, first, the use of an absolute rather than a percentage interpolating technique for obtaining the 1948 civilian labor force, and second, the use of a nationwide index of employment rather than a purely local one.

First: absolute interpolation. This was the simplest method of getting the 1948 labor force estimate, and, the magnitude of the computational task being what it was, simplicity was an important consideration. The question which its use brings up concerns the extent to which such estimates tend to be different from those obtained by using an obviously more satisfactory percentage interpolation technique. To find the answer to this question the thirty-two area random sample (used in several of the Chapter II investigations) was employed: the 1948 civilian labor force estimates were remade using percentage interpolation,[18] and the differences between these estimates and those found by using absolute interpolation were obtained; for each area, this difference was expressed as a percentage of the smaller estimate—which was always the percentage estimate, except when the two were equal. In twenty-four of the thirty-two areas the difference between the estimates was less than *ten workers*. In only one labor market area was the difference between the two estimates as great as *1 per cent;* the mean of the percentage differences for the whole sample was two-tenths of 1 per cent. Thus the magnitude of error in this connection appears generally to be quite small.

Second: the nationwide unemployment index. The desirability of using a nationwide index of unemployment is implicit in all that was said in Section 2, of Chapter II, "Transitory Elements in the Classification of Firms by Employment in March, 1948." There the main point of emphasis was that concentration ratios should reflect the "permanent"

18. The percentage interpolation procedure was as follows: the logarithms of the 1940 and 1950 civilian labor forces were found; the difference between them was multiplied by two-tenths; this product was deducted from or added to the logarithm of the 1950 civilian labor force depending on whether the 1950 civilian labor force was, respectively, greater than or less than the 1940 civilian labor force; the antilogarithm of the result was the desired estimate for 1948.

concentration situation as it exists in local labor market areas. Or, to put it the other way around, the concentration ratios should not reflect transitory concentration influences. That such transitory elements are very much a part of the best employment data available for this period can quickly and easily be seen by looking at the unemployment maps of the United States prepared by the Bureau of Employment Security. These maps show the various state unemployment averages (as percentages of state employment) by means of shadings and cross-hatchings.[19] The change in these map markings from month to month during, say, the year before and after March, 1948, is a continuous one; this widespread change in the monthly averages strongly re-enforces the belief that the use of county-by-county averages as they exist at any point in time would result in the incorporation into the data of many highly transitory factors.

The use of an area-by-area type of adjustment would be justified only if there were reason to believe that there were persistent tendencies for the "stabilized" level of unemployment in the various areas to differ. No serious effort was made to discover the extent to which there were "pockets" of local area unemployment which differed in a consistent fashion from the national level. The fact that the whole post-World War II period has been one of intense business activity

TABLE 36
FREQUENCY DISTRIBUTION OF STATES BY
PERCENTAGE OF UNEMPLOYED
(MARCH, 1948)[a]

Percentage Unemployed[b]	Number of States[c]
1.0-1.9	3
2.0-2.9	17
3.0-3.9	12
4.0-4.9	8
5.0-5.9	7
6.0-6.9	1
7.0-7.9	1

[a] Source: U.S., Federal Security Agency, Social Security Administration, Bureau of Employment Security, "Employment Security Activities," April, 1948, Vol. IV, No. 4, pp. 4-6 (Processed).
[b] Ratios of state insured unemployment for week ending March 13, 1948, to average employment covered by state unemployment insurance laws.
[c] Includes Washington, D.C., as a separate state.

19. These maps may be found in the Bureau of Employment Security's processed monthly summaries of activities which, at that time, were designated "Employment Security Activities."

TABLE 37

SELECTED DATA INDICATING RELATIVELY HIGH PERCENTAGE OF
NOT-SKILLED WORKERS IN LARGE-FIRM INDUSTRY GROUPS

Industry Group	Large[a] Firms as a Percentage of All Firms in the Industry[b]	Large[a] Firms, This Industry, as a Percentage of All-Industry Total of Large Firms[b]	Not-skilled[c] as a Percentage of Total Industry Employment[d]	Total Employment, This Industry, as a Percentage of All-Industry Total Employment[d]	Not-skilled,[c] This Industry, as a Percentage of All-Industry Not-skilled[d]
(1)	(2)	(3)	(4)	(5)	(6)
All industries	1.7	100.0	60.9	100.0	100.0
Selected industries					
Mining	6.0	3.7	75.0	1.7	2.0
Manufacturing	9.2	54.3	70.8	25.9	30.1
Public utilities[e]	3.6	7.8	68.1	7.8	8.7
Total, selected industries	—[f]	65.8	70.4[g]	35.3[h]	40.9[h]

[a] Firms hiring 100 or more workers.
[b] U.S., Department of Commerce, *1948 County Business Patterns*, Part I, pp. 10-11.
[c] Not-skilled, for purposes of these computations, is defined as the total employed labor force less the employed workers in the following census categories:
   1. Professional, Technical, and Kindred Workers.
   2. Managers, Officials, and Proprietors, Including Farm.
   3. Craftsmen, Foremen, and Kindred Workers.
[d] U.S., Bureau of the Census, *1950 Census of Population: Detailed Characteristics*, Preprint of Volume II, Part I, Chapter C, pp. 282-83.
[e] Railroads are not included so the figures in columns (2) and (3) are probably too small.
[f] Statistic not computed.
[g] Computed by dividing summed not-skilled employment of the selected industries into summed total employment of these industries.
[h] Rounding error.

and widespread reallocation of economic resources—most
especially manpower—may be relied upon to set very rigid
upper limits to the possible error resulting from the lack of
an area-by-area unemployment study.

In any event, Table 36 shows that the state unemployment
percentages clustered heavily around the figure used in the
computations (3.6), thus supporting the notion that the use of
the national average does little violence to the situation in
most labor market areas.

8. FURTHER CONCENTRATION RATIO DETAILS

The Bias in Overall Concentration Ratios

It was pointed out in Section 1 of Chapter II that Overall
concentration ratios tend to understate the actual concentration situation existing in the not-skilled portion of labor markets. This conclusion is derived from the tendency for not-

skilled workers to be distributed disproportionately toward large firms, as shown in Table 37.

Columns (2) and (3) of the table, based upon BOASI data, constitute the basis for the selection of mining, manufacturing, and public utilities as large-firm industry groups. These were the only three industry groups containing a larger percentage of firms hiring 100 or more workers than the all-industry average; and their combined large firms constituted almost two-thirds of the all-industry total. The remaining columns are based on census data. Column (4) shows the percentage of not-skilled workers in the large-firm industry groups to be 70.4, which is considerably larger than the all-industry average of 60.9 per cent. Columns (5) and (6) give a different view of the same picture. They show that these industry groups contain 35.3 per cent of the total employed labor force but 40.8 per cent of the not-skilled labor force. Both ways of looking at the occupational structure of these industry groups (by comparing 70.4 per cent with 60.9 per cent or by comparing 40.8 per cent with 35.3 per cent) lead toward the conclusion that the Overall concentration ratios will tend to understate concentration in the not-skilled labor market by about 16 per cent.[20]

Deleting Farm Workers from Maximum Denominators

It was pointed out in Section 1 of Chapter II that present understanding of the interactions between the farm and nonfarm components of the labor market are not great enough to permit a sure judgment on the desirability of removing farm workers from Maximum denominators. Some notion of the possible error involved in deleting them may be gained by reference to aggregate data. The not-skilled as defined for these estimates total 31.8 million employed workers in 1950 for the United States as a whole. If the two groups of farm labor had been included, this total would have risen by 2.4 million—an increase of 7.5 per cent. It is this calculation

20. The above analysis has proceeded by pointing out that the not-skilled tend to be distributed disproportionately toward large-firm industries. The procedure could, of course, be reversed easily by demonstrating that industries typically thought of as small-firm industries contain disproportionately higher numbers of skilled workers. Thus the same data sources show agriculture, wholesale and retail trade, business and repair services, and construction (a) contain 49.5 per cent skilled workers in comparison with the all-industry average of 39.1 per cent, and (b) contain 39.8 per cent of the total employed labor force but 50.3 per cent of the employed skilled workers.

that underlies the estimate provided in the text. Maximum concentration ratios would decrease by about 7 per cent if these agricultural workers were brought back into the denominators by distributing them uniformly among all areas—by distributing them in proportion to the areas' non-farm employed work forces.

More specific information as to the nature of the possible error in the Maximum estimates—both as to their accuracy for indicating the level of concentration and for ranking areas according to concentration—was obtained from a sample drawn at random from the high concentration region of the areas arrayed by concentration. A machine tabulation was used; it consisted of a listing of all 1,774 areas by concentration (as indicated by the ratios for the single largest employers, the Maximum-1 ratios), from lowest to highest. A number between zero and twelve was chosen at random: it was eight. So the eighth area from the "top" of the listing and every eleventh area thereafter (counting "down" the tabulation from "high" to "low" concentration) were drawn until a total of twenty-five areas had been selected. This procedure provided a sample drawn from the "highest" 15 per cent of the areas; about one-third of the sample (eight areas) was thus drawn from that portion of the areas given special attention in Chapter III—the "top" 5 per cent areas—and the other two-thirds of the sample came from those areas immediately below these in concentration.

For each area in the sample the revised Maximum-1 concentration ratio (the employment of the single largest firm divided by the Maximum denominator) was computed by including the farm categories in the denominator; all of these revised estimates were, of course, smaller than the original estimates. For each area the difference between the two percentages was obtained and expressed as a percentage of the original estimates. The resulting percentage differentials indicate the degree of "overstatement" of concentration in the original Maximum estimates. The average of the differentials for the twenty-five area sample was 10.5 per cent. It would be expected that this figure would be larger than the 7 per cent figure obtained by the use of aggregate data for, as shown in Chapter III, the larger population centers in which the proportion of farm labor is relatively low typically have "low" concentration ratios.

Finally, the areas in the sample were ranked by their original Maximum-1 concentration ratios and by the revised Maximum-1 ratios. The Spearman rank coefficient of correlation was +.9469. None of the eight areas which were drawn from the "top" 5 per cent region of the array was displaced in the process of reranking the areas by revised Maximum-1 concentration ratios.

Thus it appears that the inclusion of agricultural workers in the denominators of Maximum estimates of concentration would have lowered the concentration ratios of most of the high concentration areas by about 11 per cent but would have had little effect upon their relative concentration positions.

9. LABOR MARKET AREAS

There are certain problems relating to the labor market areas of this study which require special note. It is the purpose of this section to describe these problems and to indicate the ways they were resolved. These aims are primarily accomplished in the first of its three parts, immediately below. The other two parts ("Metropolitan Areas" and "Non-Metropolitan Area Combinations of Counties") are mainly concerned with detailed descriptions of the procedures used in the construction of certain multi-county labor market areas.

Local Labor Market Areas: Definitional Problems

In the text[21] the problem of defining the geographic extent of labor markets for operational purposes was handled along these lines: two employers should be put in the same "labor market" if the suppliers of labor view the two as excellent substitutes and in different labor markets if the two are viewed by suppliers as poor substitutes. In general, counties are so small[22] that daily commuting of an employee, to a place of employment located in any portion of the county in which the employee lives, is easy physically and feasible economically—"adequate" transportation facilities exist and the cost of using them for commuting purposes is "low" relative to daily

21. See Section 1, Chapter 2.
22. See U.S. Bureau of the Census, *Sixteenth Census of the United States: 1940. Areas of the United States*, p. 4. Changes made between 1940 and 1950 (the consolidation of two counties in South Dakota, the creation of a new county in New Mexico, and the establishment of three new independent cities in Virginia) would produce only minor changes in these data.

earnings.[23] Thus the use of counties as labor market areas typically will not provide areas which are "too large"—in fact, the error will generally be in the other direction, causing concentration to be overstated.

This approach is surely satisfactory, but a question may be raised concerning the expressions "typically," "in general," etc.; their role in the above paragraph is that of allowing for the possibility that the very large areas *are* "too large." Should some effort be made to draw a line somewhere along the county size continuum indicating the maximum size, in terms of square miles, over which firms could be scattered and still be thought of as excellent employment substitutes by potential suppliers of labor? Such a blanket "physical" solution to what is fundamentally a highly variable economic problem would obviously leave much to be desired, so the issue was approached from another direction. This question was raised: Do the concentration data themselves indicate that the "size" of the areas is such as to "hide" concentration—to obscure the existence of concentration in counties which, if appropriately subdivided, would be seen to contain local labor market areas high in actual concentration? There are 260 counties over 2,000 square miles in area in the United States; most of these are in the eight Mountain states of Montana, Idaho, Wyoming, Colorado, New Mexico, Arizona, Utah, and Nevada. Of the 278 counties (including Yellowstone National Park) in these states, 132 met the criterion for inclusion in this study. Preliminary examination of the data for these areas showed counties of these states to be high in concentration in comparison with the counties of states in other geographic sections of the country; moreover, some of the very large counties of the Mountain region were especially high in concentration. It appeared to be clear, then, that the situation in at least some of these areas was such that the large number of square miles did not preclude the appearance of concentration; therefore, it was decided that the meaningfulness of the study would be increased

23. This statement's validity is supported not so much by such statistics as the number of miles of paved highways in the United States as by evidence showing that widespread commuting is a routine feature of American labor market participation. See, as an example of this evidence: Leonard P. Adams and Thomas W. Mackesey, *Commuting Patterns of Industrial Workers: A Study of Experience Since 1940 in the Northeast Region* (Ithaca, N.Y.: Housing Research Center, Cornell University, 1955).

by the inclusion of all counties, however large, which met the basic criterion for consideration.

A problem highly comparable with the one discussed above grew out of the fact that the county coding system of the Bureau of Old-Age and Survivors Insurance provides for a maximum of ninety-nine counties in any one state. Eight states, Georgia, Illinois, Kansas, Kentucky, Missouri, North Carolina, Texas, and Virginia, contain more than ninety-nine counties; consequently, some counties are combined in Old-Age and Survivors Insurance tabulations. The case of Georgia, cited in the text, may helpfully be restated here: it contained 159 counties in all; 66 of these were presented separately and 93 of them were grouped into thirty-three units of two or more contiguous counties. The problem which arose was whether to discard the combined areas or to accept them and incorporate them into the study as single-county units. The only state in which the resulting combinations were such as to put them in the "very large" category was Texas. There one combination resulted in an area of almost 25,000 square miles; others over 5,000 square miles in area were established. No reason was seen to differentiate these "large" areas from those of the Mountain states, so they were included within the scope of the study, to the extent that they, as multi-county units, met the at-least-one-large-firm criterion for inclusion.

The definitions and data sources of this paper make it necessary to recognize a situs problem. That is, it may be assumed that there are many workers who commute across the boundaries of local labor market areas as they are defined herein. This constitutes a problem because the numerators of concentration ratios (employer data based on Bureau of Old-Age and Survivors Insurance tabulations) place workers in the same county as the business firm by which they are employed. The denominators (census employment estimates) place workers in the counties in which their residences are located. Hence, concentration tends to be overstated in those counties which have a net inflow of workers and understated in those counties experiencing a net outflow of workers. This almost surely means that most of the concentration ratios of this paper are in error to some degree. However, since most workers live within a few miles of their places of work and since much cross-county-line commuting may be presumed to be offset, with respect to its influence upon concentration, by counter flows of commuting workers, the areas for which serious misrepresentation of concentration is probable are confined to two types: those counties which constitute a portion of a large metropolitan area, and those which have relatively large cities on or near their borders.

The sorts of problems presented by areas which constitute a part of a metropolitan area may be illustrated by the counties of Fairfax, Virginia, and Schenectady, New York. In the former, BOASI sources indicate that a total of 2,852 workers were employed by covered firms in March, 1948, whereas an estimate of the residential labor force of approximately the same date was 28,598. The presumption seems established that Fairfax was at that time primarily a residential area supplying workers to the Washington, D.C., metropolitan area. Schenectady, New York, represents the opposite sort of case. There the number of workers employed in firms covered by OASI was 57,904, whereas the census estimate, based on location of residence, was 55,942. Clearly, this county was a labor-receiving one. These areas are extreme cases: most of the counties that make up metropolitan areas do not show such discrepancies between the numbers of residential and non-residential workers. However, these illustrations do serve the purpose of pointing up the fact that such areas are not areas in which it is acceptable to assume that cross-county labor flows can be discounted as minor sources of error.

In recognition of the need for data concerned with the totality of metropolitan areas, the Bureau of the Census, in collaboration with several other federal agencies, developed standard metropolitan areas for use in the 1950 Census, and the "metropolitan areas" of this study are, with a few minor modifications, these. A standard metropolitan area consists of one or more central cities of 50,000 population or over and contiguous areas that are socially and economically integrated with it. Most of these areas comprise one or more whole counties; this feature gives them more general usefulness than the metropolitan districts of the 1940 Census, because many types of data—such as the BOASI employer data used herein —are available only on a county basis. The standard metropolitan areas that are not drawn to conform to county lines are all in New England[24]—it was necessary to redraw these

24. U.S. Bureau of the Census, *1950 Census of Population: General Characteristics, U.S. Summary*, vii.

in order to make them comparable with the BOASI data. Since the census areas were not used without alteration,[25] the urban concentrations of this study are referred to simply as "metropolitan areas"; 45 of them consist of two or more counties and 115 are single-county units.

The other sort of situation in which large error may result from commuting involves those counties with relatively large cities near their borders. To illustrate, consider the hypothetical case of County "A" with a single large city close to its border; one-half of the labor force working in the city commutes from adjacent County "B" which is predominately agricultural. If concentration ratios for these counties were determined using residential labor forces, the extent of actual concentration would be overstated in "A" and understated in "B." Twenty-three pairs of counties, in which the above sort of situation seemed likely, were found; these were combined into twenty-three non-metropolitan area combinations.[26]

There were two other combination problems. The first was necessitated by the creation of a new county, Los Alamos, New Mexico, between 1940 and 1950.[27] The second involved the independent cities of Virginia. (Other independent cities were parts of standard metropolitan areas.) Data for these Virginia cities were provided separately in the census sources but, in the Bureau of Old-Age and Survivors Insurance tabulations, they were combined with appropriate counties. The Bureau of Old-Age and Survivors Insurance city-county combinations were used.

Metropolitan Areas

The metropolitan areas of this paper consist primarily of standard metropolitan areas as defined in the 1950 Census. A few minor definitional changes were made in the census areas outside of New England to increase comparability with Bureau of Old-Age and Survivors Insurance data; these changes are described in the final portion of this subsection. Much more important were the changes necessitated in the New England definitions, which were unacceptable for pur-

25. A detailed description of the modifications of standard metropolitan areas in New England is presented in the following part of this section. Some slight redefinition of three standard metropolitan areas outside New England was necessary, and these alterations are described in the following part also.

26. The criteria used in the selection of counties for combination and the procedures used in locating them are outlined in the last part of this section.

27. See the last part of this section.

poses of this study because county lines were not used as boundaries. "In New England, the city and town are administratively more important than the county, and data are compiled locally for such minor civil divisions. Here towns and cities were the units used in defining standard metropolitan areas. . . ."[28] It was decided to redefine these census areas in such a fashion as to make their boundaries coincide with county lines because the Bureau of Old-Age and Survivors Insurance data, from which concentration ratio numerators were determined, were classified in New England, as in other parts of the United States, by county.

Metropolitan Areas in New England

The Bureau of the Census Committee on Statistical Areas sponsored a project requiring the redelineation of standard metropolitan areas along county lines, which was completed in time for use in the 1950 Census. This project had as its aim the establishment of a new set of geographic areas, intermediate in size between counties and states, which have similar economic and social characteristics; they were called "state economic areas." The metropolitan area problem was handled by these project workers largely by accepting the standard metropolitan areas, redesignated "metropolitan state economic areas," as their basic metropolitan units: ". . . to establish the metropolitan economic areas, the larger standard metropolitan areas . . . were adopted without alteration except in New England."[29] In New England the metropolitan state economic areas were established along county lines, and the attempt was made to approximate the corresponding standard metropolitan areas as closely as possible. Standard metropolitan areas with less than 100,000 population in 1940 or at the time of some subsequent special census were not established as metropolitan state economic areas.

There were two potential sources of difficulty in the use of metropolitan state economic areas as the metropolitan areas of this study. The first of these lay in the fact that some small standard metropolitan areas were not designated as

28. U.S. Bureau of the Census, *1950 Census of Population: U.S. Summary, Number of Inhabitants,* p. xxxi. All 1950 population data presented throughout this subsection were obtained from the P-A series of preprints of Vol. I.

29. Donald J. Bogue, *State Economic Areas: A Description Used in Making a Functional Grouping of the Counties of the United States* (Washington: U.S. Government Printing Office, 1951), p. 6. All statements relating to metropolitan state economic areas throughout this subsection are based upon this publication.

metropolitan state economic areas; the second lay in the fact that metropolitan state economic areas do not cross state lines. With respect to New England, then, it was decided: (a) that all metropolitan state economic areas including standard metropolitan areas no part of which crossed state lines would be accepted as metropolitan areas if there were no readily apparent conflicts between the metropolitan state economic area definitions and the aims of this research effort; (b) that all metropolitan state economic areas including standard metropolitan areas parts of which lay across state lines would be given critical examination before acceptance as metropolitan areas; (c) that, in order to promote nationwide uniformity of metropolitan areas, any standard metropolitan areas not converted into metropolitan state economic areas because of the 100,000 population criterion would be included as metropolitan areas after being redefined along county lines.

There are eighteen standard metropolitan areas in the New England geographic division. Seventeen of these were incorporated into eleven metropolitan state economic areas, all of which were found to be acceptable as metropolitan areas for purposes of this study; the twelfth metropolitan area consists of a county which included one standard metropolitan area that was not large enough to qualify as a metropolitan state economic area. The detailed reasoning underlying the metropolitan area table (Table 38) is discussed under the following headings: intrastate boundary problems, interstate boundary problems, and "small" standard metropolitan areas.

Intrastate Boundary Problems.—The first three metropolitan areas in the accompanying table are single-county units each of which includes a complete standard metropolitan area. That is, no portions of the Manchester, New Hampshire, Portland, Maine, and Worcester, Massachusetts, standard metropolitan areas lie outside the relevant counties that serve as the definitions of the corresponding metropolitan state economic areas; in these cases there is no question about the fact that the metropolitan state economic area definitions are appropriate for this study.

The Brockton, Massachusetts, metropolitan area consists of Massachusetts metropolitan state economic area "D" which, in turn, includes most of the Brockton standard metropolitan area in addition to the rest of Plymouth County,

Massachusetts. The use of county lines as metropolitan
boundaries necessitates making that part of the Brockton
standard metropolitan area which was in Norfolk County
(the towns of Avon, Holbrook, and Stoughton, combined 1950
population, 17,786) a part of the Boston-Lowell-Lawrence
metropolitan area, and that part of the Brockton standard
metropolitan area which was in Bristol County (the town of
Easton, 1950 population, 6,244) a part of the Fall River–New
Bedford, Massachusetts, metropolitan area. The same factor
makes it necessary to take the towns of Hingham and Hull
(combined 1950 population, 14,044) in Plymouth County out
of the Boston-Lowell-Lawrence area and place them in the
Brockton metropolitan area. The use of the metropolitan
state economic area definition in this case keeps the Brockton
standard metropolitan area largely intact and so represents
the best way that the area can be incorporated into this study.

The next two metropolitan areas in the table are multiple-
county units that result from the fact that significant proportions of single standard metropolitan areas lie across county
lines. The total population of the Springfield-Holyoke standard metropolitan area was about 400,000 in 1950; most of the
inhabitants lived in Hampden County but approximately one-
eighth lived in Hampshire; hence the metropolitan state economic area was defined as both of these counties, a definition
consistent with the aims and the procedures of this study.
The Boston-Lowell-Lawrence metropolitan area definition
represents a solution to a comparable problem. In this case
the metropolitan state economic area definition includes three
distinct standard metropolitan areas. The Lowell and Law-
rence standard metropolitan areas are merged with the Boston standard metropolitan area because other portions of the
counties in which these two standard metropolitan areas are
situated (Middlesex and Essex) are integral parts of the
Boston standard metropolitan area. In each case, the proportion of the county's population in the Boston standard metropolitan area in 1950 was much greater than that in the other
standard metropolitan area.

The Providence, Rhode Island, metropolitan area consists
of Bristol, Kent, and Providence counties; its definition is
identical with that of Rhode Island metropolitan state economic area "A." The standard metropolitan area which corresponds to this metropolitan state economic area includes

TABLE 38. COMPARISON OF METROPOLITAN AREAS AS
ECONOMIC AREAS AND STANDARD

Metropolitan Area		Metropolitan State Economic Area[a]	
Designation	Definition	Designation	Definition
1. Manchester, N.H.	Hillsborough County, N.H.	New Hampshire Metropolitan Area A	Hillsborough County, N.H.
2. Portland, Me.	Cumberland County, Me.	Maine Metropolitan Area A	Cumberland County, Me.
3. Worcester, Mass.	Worcester County, Mass.	Massachusetts Metropolitan Area B	Worcester County, Mass.
4. Brockton, Mass.	Plymouth County, Mass.	Massachusetts Metropolitan Area D	Plymouth County, Mass.
5. Springfield-Holyoke, Mass.	Hampshire and Hampden counties, Mass.	Massachusetts Metropolitan Area A	Hampden and Hampshire counties, Mass.
6. Boston-Lawrence-Lowell, Mass.	Essex, Middlesex, Norfolk, and Suffolk counties, Mass.	Massachusetts Metropolitan Area C	Essex, Middlesex, Norfolk, and Suffolk counties, Mass.
7. Providence, R.I.	Bristol, Kent, and Providence counties, R.I.	Rhode Island Metropolitan Area A	Bristol, Kent, and Providence counties, R.I.
8. Fall River-New Bedford, Mass.	Bristol County, Mass.	Massachusetts Metropolitan Area E	Bristol County, Mass.
9. Hartford-New Britain-Bristol, Conn.	Hartford County, Conn.	Connecticut Metropolitan Area C	Hartford County, Conn
10. Waterbury-New Haven, Conn.	New Haven County, Conn.	Connecticut Metropolitan Area B	New Haven County, Conn.
11. Bridgeport-Stamford-Norwalk, Conn.	Fairfield County, Conn.	Connecticut Metropolitan Area A	Fairfield County, Conn.
12. Pittsfield, Mass.	Berkshire County, Mass.	None	None

[a] Donald J. Bogue, *State Economic Areas: A Description Used in Making a Functional Grouping of the Counties of the United States* (Washington: U.S. Government Printing Office, 1951), pp. 81-96.

only portions of Providence and Kent counties. It includes
the additional town of North Kingstown in Washington

DEFINED FOR THIS STUDY WITH METROPOLITAN STATE
METROPOLITAN AREAS, IN NEW ENGLAND

Standard Metropolitan Area[b]	
Designation	Definition
Manchester, N.H.	Manchester city and Goffstown town in Hillsborough County, N.H.
Portland, Me.	Portland, South Portland, and Westbrook cities; Cape Elizabeth and Falmouth towns in Cumberland County, Me.
Worcester, Mass.	Worcester city; Auburn, East Brookfield, Grafton, Holden, Leicester, Millbury, Northborough, North Brookfield, Shrewsbury, Spencer, Westborough, and West Boylston towns in Worcester County, Mass.
Brockton, Mass.	Brockton city; Abington, Bridgewater, East Bridgewater, Rockland, West Bridgewater, and Whitman towns in Plymouth County, Mass.; Avon, Holbrook, and Strughton towns in Norfolk county, Mass.; Easton town in Bristol County, Mass.
Springfield-Holyoke, Mass.	Chicopee, Holyoke, Springfield, and Westfield cities; Agawam, East Longmeadow, Longmeadow, Ludlow, West Springfield, and Wilbraham towns in Hampden County, Mass.; Northampton city; Easthampton, and South Hadley towns in Hampshire County, Mass.; Enfield town in Hartford County, Conn.
Boston, Mass.	All of Suffolk County, Mass.; Cambridge, Everett, Malden, Medford, Melrose, Newton, Somerville, Waltham, and Woburn cities; Arlington, Ashland, Bedford, Belmont, Burlington, Concord, Framingham, Lexington, Lincoln, Natick, North Reading, Reading, Soneham, Wakefield, Watertown, Wayland, Weston, Wilmington, and Winchester towns in Middlesex County, Mass.; Quincy city; Braintree, Brookline, Canton, Cohasset, Dedham, Dover, Medfield, Milton, Needham, Norwood, Randolph, Sharon, Walpole, Wellesley, Westwood, and Weymouth towns in Norfolk County, Mass.;
Lawrence, Mass. Lowell, Mass.	Lawrence city; Andover, Methuen, and North Andover towns in Essex County, Mass.; Lowell city; Billerica, Chelmsford, Dracut, and Tewksbury towns in Middlesex County, Mass.
Providence, R.I.	Central Falls, Cranston, Pawtucket, Providence, and Woonsocket cities; Cumberland, East Providence, Johnston, Lincoln, North Providence, North Smithfield, and Smithfield towns in Providence County, R. I.; North Kingstown town in Washington County, R. I.; Warwick city; East Greenwich, and West Warwick towns in Kent County, R. I.; all of Bristol County, R. I.; Attleboro city; North Attleboro, and Seekonk towns in Bristol County, Mass.; Bellingham, Franklin, Plainville, and Wrentham towns in Norfolk County, Mass.; Blackstone and Millville towns in Worcester County, Mass.
Fall River, Mass., and New Bedford, Mass.	Fall River city; Somerset, Swansea and Westport towns in Bristol County, Mass.; Tiverton town in Newport County, R. I. New Bedford city; Acushnet, Dartmouth and Fairhaven towns in Bristol County, Mass.
Hartford, Conn., and New Britain-Bristol, Conn.	Hartford city; Avon, Bloomfield, East Hartford, Farmington, Glastonbury, Manchester, Newington, Rocky Hill, Simsbury, South Windsor, West Hartford, Wethersfield, and Windsor towns in Hartford County, Conn. Bristol and New Britain cities; Berlin, Plainville and Southington towns in Hartford County, Conn.; Plymouth town in Litchfield County, Conn.
Waterbury, Conn., and New Haven, Conn.	Waterbury city; Nagatuck borough, Beacon Falls, Cheshire, Middlebury, Prospect, and Wolcott towns in New Haven County, Conn., Thomastown and Watertown towns in Litchfield County, Conn. New Haven city; Branford, East Haven, Hamden, North Haven, Orange, West Haven, and Woodbridge towns in New Haven County, Conn.
Bridgeport, Conn., and Stamford-Norwalk, Conn.	Bridgeport city; Fairfield, Stratford, and Trumbull towns in Fairfield County, Conn.; Milford town in New Haven County, Conn.; Norwalk and Stamford cities; Darien, Greenwich, New Canaan, and Westport towns in Fairfield County, Conn.
Pittsfield, Mass.	Pittsfield city; and Dalton, Lenox, and Lee towns in Berkshire County, Mass.

[b] U.S. Bureau of the Census, *United States Census of Population: 1950. General Characteristics*, Series P-B preprints of Vol. II (Washington: U.S. Government Printing Office, 1952).

County; this town (1950 population, 14,810) was dropped
from the metropolitan state economic area definition in pref-

erence to including the whole county (1950 population, 48,542)
in which it is located. The Providence standard metropolitan
area also includes areas outside the state of Rhode Island;
this boundary problem is discussed in the next portion of this
subsection.

The next three metropolitan areas in the table are single-
county units that contain all or nearly all of two standard
metropolitan areas. In the case of the first of these, Fall
River-New Bedford, Massachusetts, Bristol County contains
almost all of the two standard metropolitan areas, Fall River
and New Bedford. All of New Bedford is in Bristol and only
the town of Tilverton (population, 5,649 in 1950) of the Fall
River standard metropolitan area is outside that county; as
in other comparable cases, it was excluded in preference to
including the whole county (Newport) in which it is located.
Hence, the metropolitan area chosen for this study is Bristol
County; it is identical with Massachusetts metropolitan state
economic area "E."

The Hartford-New Britain-Bristol, Connecticut, metropolitan area consists of Hartford County which contains all
of the Hartford, Connecticut, standard metropolitan area and
the major portion of New Britain-Bristol standard metropolitan area. The only part of the latter area outside Hartford
is the town of Plymouth (6,771 population in 1950) in Litchfield County. The exclusion of this town provides a metropolitan area identical with Connecticut metropolitan state
economic area "B," which is acceptable for purposes of this
study.

New Haven County contains all of the New Haven, Connecticut, standard metropolitan area and all of the Water-
bury, Connecticut, standard metropolitan area except the
towns of Thomastown (1950 population, 4,896) and Waterton
(1950 population, 10,699) in Litchfield County, Connecticut.
This county is, then, the defined area of the Waterbury-New
Haven, Connecticut, metropolitan area; it is identical with
Connecticut metropolitan state economic area "B."

The next metropolitan area in the table, Bridgeport-
Stamford-Norwalk, Connecticut, presents the same sort of
situation as those immediately above. That is, all of the
Stamford-Norwalk, Connecticut, standard metropolitan area
and all but one town, Milford, of the Bridgeport, Connecticut,
standard metropolitan area are located within Fairfield

County in Connecticut, so the metropolitan area and the corresponding metropolitan state economic area are both defined as consisting of Fairfield County.

Interstate Boundary Problems.—The above considerations make it clear that the metropolitan state economic area definitions are acceptable standard metropolitan area approximations for purposes of this study in so far as they are concerned with intrastate boundaries. However, standard metropolitan areas were drawn without consideration of state boundaries whereas metropolitan state economic areas were not permitted to cross state lines. It was necessary, therefore, to examine all metropolitan state economic areas with a view toward determining if this restriction made for any unsatisfactory metropolitan area definitions. In New England, there are five counties that have some portions as parts of a standard metropolitan area located predominately across a state line. In four of these cases, another portion of the individual counties involved includes, or is a part of, another standard metropolitan area. In these four cases, it was decided that the intrastate ties of the counties concerned were more significant than those with standard metropolitan areas across state lines; hence, no alterations in the metropolitan state economic area delineations were made. In the fifth county the portion of the county included in a standard metropolitan area of another state was deemed too small to warrant the inclusion of the whole county.

The detailed data and decisions underlying the above general statements follow:

1. Portions of Norfolk, Bristol, and Worcester counties in Massachusetts are parts of the Providence, Rhode Island, standard metropolitan area.

A. Including Norfolk County in the Providence, Rhode Island, metropolitan area would mean excluding it from the Boston metropolitan area. Casual observation of the relevant census map indicates that such action would be undesirable. This tentative conclusion is confirmed by reference to 1950 population figures; the four Norfolk towns in the Providence standard metropolitan area had a combined population of less than one-fourth that of the largest of the several Norfolk urban centers in the Boston standard metropolitan area.

B. Bristol County, Massachusetts, includes all of the New Bedford standard metropolitan area and most of the Fall

River standard metropolitan area. Both of these standard metropolitan areas would be included within the Providence, Rhode Island, metropolitan area if that metropolitan area were redefined as to include Bristol County. Acceptance of the metropolitan state economic area definition of Bristol County as a metropolitan area, however, involves a less drastic violation of standard metropolitan area definitions: specifically, it involves including Attleboro, North Attleboro, and the town of Seeking (combined 1950 population, approximately 42,000), which are a part of the Providence standard metropolitan area, in the Bristol metropolitan area.

C. Two towns, Blackstone and Millville, in Worcester County, Massachusetts, are included within the Providence, Rhode Island, standard metropolitan area. Bringing these two towns (combined 1950 population, 6,660) into the Providence metropolitan area by including the whole of Worcester County would have involved the inclusion of the separate and distinct Worcester standard metropolitan area (1950 population, 276,336) in the Providence metropolitan area also. In order to preserve the identity of this standard metropolitan area, Worcester County was defined as a metropolitan area for purposes of this study; it was not incorporated into the Providence metropolitan area.

2. The case of Hartford County in Connecticut is the same as that of Worcester. That is, a small portion of this county (the town of Enfield, 1950 population, 15,464) is included in the Springfield-Holyoke, Massachusetts, standard metropolitan area; the inclusion of the whole of Hartford County within the Springfield-Holyoke metropolitan area would have meant the loss of identity of the separate and distinct Hartford and New Britain-Bristol standard metropolitan areas. Therefore, Hartford County was designated a metropolitan area for purposes of this paper.

3. Finally, the town of Tilverton in Newport County, Rhode Island, is included within the Fall River, Massachusetts, standard metropolitan area. The definitional question here was whether or not to include the whole of Newport County in the Bristol metropolitan area (which includes both the Fall River and New Bedford standard metropolitan areas). Since Tilverton had a 1950 population of only 5,659, it was decided that deleting this town would be preferable to

bringing all of Newport County (1950 population, 61,539) into the Bristol metropolitan area.

"Small" Standard Metropolitan Area Problems.—The final aspect of converting standard metropolitan areas into metropolitan areas involved checking to see if any standard metropolitan areas were not converted into metropolitan state economic areas because of the 100,000 population criterion. It was found that the Pittsfield, Massachusetts, standard metropolitan area (1950 population, 66,567) was the only standard metropolitan area in New England which was excluded as a metropolitan state economic area. No portion of that standard metropolitan area is outside of Bershire County, Massachusetts; therefore, that county was adopted as a metropolitan area for purposes of this study.

Metropolitan Areas Outside New England

The preceding portion of this subsection points up the fact that New England metropolitan area definitions correspond almost completely with metropolitan state economic area definitions. With three exceptions, metropolitan areas throughout the rest of the United States are identical with standard metropolitan areas. The exceptions represent changes from the standard metropolitan area definitions necessitated by the fact that some of the counties in standard metropolitan areas were combined with other areas in the BOASI data sources. Thus the Chattanooga, Tennessee, standard metropolitan area comprises Hamilton County in Tennessee and Walker County in Georgia. But Walker County is grouped with two others, Cartoosa and Dade, for Bureau of Old-Age and Survivors Insurance data purposes, so this metropolitan area was defined to include the additional counties. Similarly, the Macon, Georgia, standard metropolitan area consists of Bibb and Houston counties, but Houston is grouped with Peach and Twiggs counties for purposes of Bureau of Old-Age and Survivors Insurance data presentation; consequently, the Macon metropolitan area was defined to include Peach and Twiggs. For exactly the same sort of reason, the Richmond, Virginia, metropolitan area was defined to include the independent city of Colonial Heights, Virginia. In all three of these cases the quantitative significance of the changes was small; all of the "extra" counties were small (in terms of population size) in comparison with the standard metropolitan areas to which they were appended.

Non-Metropolitan Area Combinations of Counties

The numerators of concentration ratios represent the combined employment of the single largest, the four largest, and the ten largest firms in labor market areas; these figures were obtained from OASI sources, which allocate workers geographically according to county of employer location. Intercounty commuting may introduce error into concentration ratios because the denominators—estimates of the employed labor force—were obtained from census sources that place workers by county of residence. Consequently, the estimates of employed workers are too large in those areas which are net exporters of commuters. The problem under consideration in this subsection is that of describing the procedures used to locate those areas, other than standard metropolitan areas, for which circumstances provide a strong presumption of appreciable error because of this factor.

As pointed out earlier in this section, standard metropolitan area definitions are assumed to be such as to have reduced the magnitude of this problem to an acceptable margin of error for all counties in which, or adjacent to which, there are one or more cities of 50,000 or greater population. The remaining task is that of examining counties containing cities of less than 50,000 population with a view toward combining those which appear to contain seriously-distorting commuting possibilities.

Generally speaking, most urban workers live within the city limits of the communities in which they work or very close to their boundary lines. This means that, unless any particular city is near the border of a county, the chances are small that a large proportion of that city's labor force will reside outside the county. Consider, for example, the case of a city, five miles from a county boundary, the non-residential labor force of which is geographically distributed more or less at random throughout the surrounding countryside. It would be expected that the density of this portion of the city's labor force would tend to vary inversely with the distance from the city limits, so that it is probable that most of the workers concerned live within a few miles of the city proper. Thus, even if the total portion of the labor force living outside the city were as high as one-third or more, the chances are great that the portion living across the county line is a small portion of the city's total labor force—and a smaller portion still of the labor force of the county in which the city is located. These sorts of considerations underlie the expectation that, unless there are special circumstances involved, a city must be fairly close to a county border for it to be a serious source of error in the estimate of the total employed labor force. Whatever error there is will be reflected in the concentration ratios of both counties concerned: that receiving the net inflow of commuting workers and that experiencing a net outflow. Just how serious the error is will depend upon the magnitude of the net flow in comparison with the sizes of the denominators.

There were no commuting data available at the time of this study which would permit accurate combination decisions to be made. Consequently, the problem was that of locating situations in which there was a reasonable probability of the existence of commuting error. This meant the task was that of seeking out cities near county borders, cities that were large in comparison with either or both of the counties involved.

The "rules" devised to serve as general guides in combining counties were as follows:

1. When the city limits are cut by the county line, the counties will be considered for combination if either of the following conditions obtain: (a) the parts of the city on both sides of the county line and the minor civil divisions (variously called townships, districts, divisions, etc.) in which they lie contain one-half of the total population of the two counties; or (b) considering each portion of the city as separate cities, either rules 2(a) or 3(a) below obtain.

2. When the city is near the border, inside the larger county, the counties will be considered for combination if either of the following conditions obtain: (a) the minor civil division in which the city is located, together with the city, contains as large a population as the smaller county, and one-half of the population of the smaller county is located in the minor civil division closest to the city; or (b) one-half of the population of the smaller county is located in the minor civil division next to the city, and the minor civil divisions on either side of the line, including the city, contain one-half of the population of the two counties together.

3. When the city is near the border, inside the smaller county, the counties will be considered for combination if either of the following conditions obtain: (a) the city, plus the minor civil division in which it is located, contains as large a population as the rest of the county, and the minor civil division directly across the line contains a population equally large; or (b) one-half the population of the smaller county is in the city and the minor civil division associated with it, and the minor civil divisions on either side of the line, including the city, contain one-half of the combined population of the two counties.

Rules 1, 2(b), and 3(b) are designed to designate pairs of counties which, considered as a unit, have a large portion of their joint population concentrated in the minor civil divisions at their common border; that is, the aim of these rules is that of recommending for combination counties which seem to have a common core, but are located partially in one area and partially in another. Rule 2 is designed to recommend for combination pairs of counties that have two characteristics: population is concentrated in the smaller county such that it is reasonable to expect a net export of commuters, and the city in the larger county is big enough in comparison with the smaller county to suggest that the commuter flow might be of such a magnitude as to cause an appreciable error in one or both of the denominators of the two counties. Rule 3 is designed to point out pairs of counties that have very slightly different characteristics: there is a concentration of population in the larger county, near the city in the smaller county, of such a magnitude that it appears that the economic relationship between the city and the region in the adjoining county is probably of greater significance than that between the city and the rest of the county in which it is located, and that, therefore, the smaller county might be a relatively sizable receiver of commuters.

In applying these rules, a city was considered to be "near the border" (of a county) if it appeared to be within a distance of about two miles of that border. Distances were not always measured, but the attempt was made to interpret distances conservatively; i.e., the rules were applied in cases which would have been excluded from examination by rigid adherence to the two-mile stipulation. Also, it was decided that cities of less than 5,000 population would not be investigated, however near the border they were located. This minimum size must be supported more by reference to research convenience than logic, for it is clear that smaller cities could be the locus of appreciable commuting error in those counties which have very small labor forces. Since, however, there were only eight areas, of the total of 1,774 actually used in this study, which had estimated total labor forces of less than 1,000, it is also clear that the possibility of important but undiscovered commuting error is not great.

Application of the criteria contained in the three rules disclosed twenty-three border-city situations that involved relatively large proportions of one or both counties in the small areas near the common border, so the forty-six counties concerned were made into twenty-three non-metropolitan area combinations.[30] It should be added that the rules were not adhered to inflexibly; they served as guides that pointed out pairs of counties between which the possibility of substantial commuting was probable. Nevertheless, most of the twenty-three combinations fitted unambiguously into one or more of the patterns described by the rules. In those cases which were accepted despite the fact that they did not conform perfectly with the patterns, it was decided that the sort of situations which the rules were designed to locate actually existed—or probably existed—but that the population magnitudes stipulated by the rules were not completely met, or that the magnitudes were obscured by the ways in which the boundaries of the minor civil divisions were drawn.

In addition to the twenty-three areas mentioned above, one other non-metropolitan area combination was made necessary by the fact that Los Alamos County, New Mexico, was created in 1949 from parts of Sandoval and Santa Fe counties, New Mexico. This presented a difficulty because 1950 data were used to determine 1948 estimates of the employed labor forces of counties; the total labor force of the area occupied by Sandoval and Santa Fe counties in 1940 was distributed among these two plus Los Alamos County in 1950. Since there was no way to allocate the 1950 Los Alamos labor

30. Cities were located by means of the state maps in the *Rand McNally Commercial Atlas and Marketing Guide*, Eighty-Third Edition, 1952 (New York: Rand McNally and Company, 1952). Application of the rules was made possible by the detailed maps (which delineate the minor civil divisions) and Table 6 ("Population of Counties by Minor Civil Divisions: 1930 to 1950"), in the U.S. Bureau of the Census, *1950 Census of Population, Number of Inhabitants*, Series P-A preprints of Vol. I.

force between the other two counties, it was decided to combine the three counties for 1950 data purposes and the two counties for 1940 data purposes, giving a single homogeneous area for the two periods. This process resulted in the twenty-fourth non-metropolitan area combination.

The twenty-three non-metropolitan area combinations are listed below alphabetically by states; in those situations in which the counties were located in different states, they were placed in the state of the larger county (as measured by size of employed labor force). The twenty-fourth combination, not in alphabetical order, is the New Mexico combination discussed immediately above.

1. Alabama: Colbert-Lauderdale
2. Arkansas: Crawford-Sebastian
3. California: Sutter-Yuba
4. Florida: Sarasota-Manatee
5. Georgia: Ware-Pierce
6. Idaho: Nez Perce-Asotin (Washington)
7. Indiana: Perry-Hancock (Kentucky)
8. Michigan: Gegobic-Iron (Wisconsin)
9. North Carolina: Rowan-Cabarrus
10. North Dakota: Cass-Clay (Minnesota)
11. North Dakota: Morton-Burleigh
12. Tennessee: Carter-Washington
13. Tennessee: Sullivan-Washington (Virginia)
14. Texas: Bowie-Miller (Arkansas)
15. Virginia: Campbell-Amherst
16. Virginia: James City-York
17. Virginia: Warwick-Elizabeth City
18. Washington: Benton-Franklin
19. Washington: Chelan-Douglas
20. Washington: Whitman-Latah (Idaho)
21. Wisconsin: Chippewa-Eau Claire
22. Wisconsin: Marinette-Monominee (Michigan)
23. Wisconsin: Outagamie-Winnebago
24. New Mexico: Sandoval-Sante Fe-Los Alamos

10. TRANSITORY ELEMENTS IN THE CONCENTRATION RATIOS

The three samples used in the two experiments briefly described in Chapter II, Section 2 were the following: the thirty-two area general random sample was a subsample, drawn from a larger (105 area) random sample used extensively in Chapter III.[31] The procedure was as follows: the designations of the areas in the larger sample were placed on index cards; these were shuffled; a random number between zero and sixteen was chosen: it was eleven; the eleventh card and every third card thereafter were selected. This technique was designed to provide a subsample of thirty or more areas; the number actually provided was thirty-two. The twenty-five area sample comprises the top twenty-five areas as ranked by Maximum-1 concentration ratios. The twenty-eight area sample comprises all areas in the 105 area sample which contained as many as ten firms hiring 100 or more workers in March, 1948. It contains three of the same areas as the thirty-two area sample, and it obviously has a large-size (in terms of employed labor force), low-concentration, bias.

The experiments performed with the samples are summarized in the accompanying tables. In the first experiment an attempt was made to find the degree of rank mobility among high-ranking firms. As shown in Table 39, all of the samples seem to be in agreement that about three-fourths of the four top-ranking firms in each area in 1948 occupied comparable rank positions in 1947. The non-availability of data confuses analysis as to the location of most of the other firms—the 25 per cent of firms which are not among the top four in 1947—but the twenty-eight area sample data suggest

31. The 105 area random sample was obtained as follows: Areas were arranged alphabetically by states. Within each state areas were arranged according to their Bureau of Old-Age and Survivors Insurance codes; these are primarily alphabetical. Non-metropolitan area combinations were placed in the appropriate state after the last county. Where two or more such combinations were located in a single state, they were arranged in alphabetical order by the first letter of the first-named county. Where such a combination crossed a state line, it was put in the state of the larger county (as measured by population size). Metropolitan areas were assigned to states by name of the last-named state; e.g., New York-Northeastern New Jersey was placed in New Jersey. Within each state, metropolitan areas were placed after non-metropolitan area combinations in alphabetical order.

A random number between zero and eighteen was chosen: it was five. The fifth area and every seventeenth area thereafter were selected. This procedure provided a 105 area sample—slightly less than 6 per cent of the total number of areas. In order to check the acceptability of this sample, a frequency distribution of the sample areas according to Overall-4 concentration ratios was compared with a similar distribution of all 1,774 areas. A chi-square test was performed; it showed a chi-square value of 7.730, which, with five degrees of freedom, shows a probability of less than 20 per cent but more than 10 per cent. This means that between 10 and 20 per cent of the time a sample this unusual would be obtained by chance; probabilities above 5 per cent are generally regarded as acceptable, so this sample was judged to be satisfactory for the purposes at hand.

TABLE 39

RANK IN 1947 OF FIRMS RANKING AMONG TOP 4
IN 1948, FOR THREE SAMPLES OF AREAS[a]

1947 Rank	Firms[b] Ranking Among Top 4 in 1948					
	In 28-Area Sample[c]		In 32-Area Sample[c]		In 25-Area Sample[c]	
	Number	Percentage	Number	Percentage	Number	Percentage
Among top 4	88	78.6	60	75.9	45	77.6
Ranking 5-10	12	10.7	4	5.1	0	0.0
Ranking below 10	1	0.9	0	0.0	0	0.0
Information not available	11	9.8	15	19.0	13	22.4
Total	112	100.0	79	100.0	58	100.0

[a] Source: The Time-Series tabulation.
[b] The Time-Series only provides information about firms hiring 100 or more employees. In March, 1948, there were some areas in the thirty-two and twenty-five area samples which did not have as many as four firms of this size. These facts explain why the thirty-two and twenty-five area sample totals are less than 128 (32 x 4) and 100 (25 x 4) respectively.
[c] For a description of the samples see accompanying text.

that at least one-half of them simply occupied lower rank positions the levels of which are unknown in the other two samples because these firms had fewer than 100 employees in 1947.[32] The chief conclusion that can be drawn from this experiment is that as many as 25 per cent of the firms that occupied a rank position among the top four firms in 1948 may have occupied a lower rank position in 1947.

The second experiment consisted of an attempt at direct measurement of the effect of transitory elements in the data upon concentration ratios. This was made possible by the fact that highly comparable concentration ratios could be computed for both 1947 and 1948 by using, for each labor market area, firm employment data as numerators (as in the Overall and Maximum ratios) and *total employment covered by the OASI program* (obtained from the *County Business Patterns* series) as denominators. For each area these inde-

32. The twenty-eight areas sample was brought into the investigation because many of the areas in the other two samples were small—small in the sense that they contained, say, only one, two, or three firms that hired as many as 100 workers. This complicated matters in two ways. First, if the firms hired only a few more than 100 workers in 1948, they would have to have only slightly fewer employees in 1947 in order not to appear on the 1947 listing—and thus appear in the ''information-not-available'' row of Table 39 above. Second, the fact that there were only a few areas in both the thirty-two and twenty-five area samples that contained as many as four firms with 100 or more employees, made it impossible to get reliable information about the transitory factor included in four-firm concentration ratios. It was to meet—at least partially—these two difficulties that this third sample of twenty-eight areas was used.

pendently computed 1947 and 1948 ratios were averaged. These averages are referred to below as the "1947-48 average ratios."

Next, combined concentration ratios were computed for all areas (independently), as follows: firms were ranked in order of their combined (summed) 1947 and 1948 employments; these two-year employment summaries were used as numerators. They were divided by the combined *total covered employment* of 1947 and 1948. These concentration ratios are referred to herein as "combined 1947-48 ratios."

In any area in which the same firms were largest in March, 1947, and March, 1948, there is a strong tendency for the 1947-48 average ratios to be equal to the combined 1947-48 ratios. On the other hand, in any area in which different firms occupy the top positions there is a strong tendency for the 1947-48 average ratio to exceed the combined 1947-48 ratios.[33] So the difference between the two measures becomes an indication of the quantitative significance of transitory influences in an area's data; expressed as a percentage of the 1947-48 average ratio, this difference is referred to herein as the "transitory differential."[34]

For all areas in all three samples, transitory differentials were computed individually for the single largest firms and, where there were enough firms with 100 employees, for the four largest firms. The sample averages of these differentials are presented in Table 40.

The average concentration data in the table suggest that the three samples may be thought of as roughly representing

33. Hypothetical illustrations can be constructed in which both of these tendencies are overcome. However, such illustrations would contain special circumstances that, as a cause of serious distortion, would be found only rarely in real-world data. That the tendencies described in the text above apply to the data of this study is indicated by an experiment performed on thirty areas of the thirty-two area general random sample for which employment data for the single-largest firm was available for 1947 and 1948. In twenty-three of these areas the same firm was largest in both years (at the mid-March date); for these areas the average of the 1947-48 average ratios was 24.27 per cent and the average of the combined 1947-48 ratios was 24.26 per cent. In the other seven areas the average of the 1947-48 average ratios was 10.05 per cent and the average of the combined 1947-48 ratios was 8.18 per cent.

34. With reference to the areas mentioned in the preceding footnote, the average of the twenty-three transitory differentials computed for the areas having the same largest firm in both years was 0.06 of 1 per cent. The average transitory differential of the seven areas for which data were available and which had different top-ranking firms in the two years was 14.64 per cent; this means that, on the average, the 1947-48 average ratios in these seven areas were greater by about 15 per cent than the combined 1947-48 ratios.

TABLE 40

ESTIMATES OF OVERSTATEMENT IN CONCENTRATION RATIOS
RESULTING FROM PRESENCE OF TRANSITORY ELEMENTS IN
FIRM EMPLOYMENT DATA, AND RELATED INFORMATION,
FOR THREE SAMPLES OF AREAS[a]

Description of Data	28 Area Sample	32 Area Sample	25 Area Sample
Simple arithmetic mean of concentration ratios[b]	13.0	19.1	61.0
Percentage of areas having same largest firm in mid-March, 1947, and 1948	67.9	71.9	84.0
Simple arithmetic mean of transitory differentials[c]			
Largest firm	5.6	5.6[d]	10.0
Four largest firms	5.7	7.1[e]	9.9[f]

[a] For a description of the samples see accompanying text.
[b] Simple arithmetic means of ratios having the employment of the areas' (single) largest firms as numerators and *total covered employments* as denominators.
[c] The transitory differential was found for each area individually by expressing the difference between the 1947-48 average ratio and the combined 1947-48 ratio as a percentage of the former.
[d] Differentials for two areas could not be computed because they contained no covered firms with as many as 100 employees in 1947. To insure overstatement of the mean, these two areas were given the largest differential occurring among the other thirty areas. If these areas had been dropped from the sample, the mean would have been 3.5.
[e] Statistic based on data from nine areas only.
[f] Statistic based on data from four areas only.

the three portions of a total distribution of all 1,774 areas by concentration: the twenty-eight area sample, with its large-size bias representing the low concentration section of the aggregate distribution, the twenty-five area sample representing the extremely high concentration section, and the thirty-two area random sample representing the region in between these two. The data on the stability of the rank position of the largest firm show, as would be expected, that the rank position of the largest firms is more secure as the relative size of those firms increases: the same firm is largest in 1947 and 1948 in approximately 68 per cent of the "low" concentration areas, 72 per cent of the "middle" concentration areas, and 84 per cent of the "very high" concentration areas. The differentials for the single largest firm concentration ratios show a high degree of constancy for the "lower" and "middle" concentration areas at about 5.6 per cent, with a rise to approximately 10 per cent among the "very high" concentration areas. Thus the transitory factor seems to alter the single largest firm concentration ratios among more low concentration areas than high, but the impact upon high concentration areas is greater.

The differentials for the four largest firm concentration ratios are much less satisfactory because so many areas drop out of two of the samples for purposes of this computation.

But such data as there are tell substantially the same story: the maximum amount of the overstatement of concentration due to the presence of transitory elements in the four largest firm concentration ratios is about 6 per cent in the lower portion of the aggregate distribution of areas by concentration and it may rise as high as 10 per cent in the very high concentration portion of that distribution.

The areas of the high concentration sample were ranked according to the 1947-48 average ratios and according to the combined 1947-48 ratios. The rank correlation coefficient which represents a comparison of these two rankings was a comfortably high +.74.[35]

35. It should be noted that all of the data were computed in such a way that the extent of the transitory problem may be overstated throughout the above discussion. This can best be shown by means of a hypothetical case. In a certain area there are two firms hiring more than 100 employees in both 1947 and 1948. Examination of the employer code numbers shows that there are only three different units: Firm A appears in both periods, with 103 workers in 1947 and 107 workers in 1948; Firm B appears in 1947 with 170 workers; Firm C appears in 1948 with 175 workers. Further investigation shows that units "B" and "C" have the same industry code numbers. In such a case, the data of Firms B and C would be used for purposes of calculating the independent concentration ratios for 1947 and 1948 from which the 1947-48 average ratio would be computed. But, since nothing is known about either of these two firms in one of the two years, both would be ruled out of consideration for the purpose of computing the combined ratio; Firm C employment data (103 plus 107) would be used as the numerator of the combined 1947-48 ratio.

This procedure admits two obvious possibilities of error. First, it may be that Firms B and C are the same unit, which unit has experienced a change in ownership during the interval between the two reporting dates in mid-March—both the employment numbers and industry classification suggest that this is the case. Second, it may be that "B" and "C" actually are different firms both of which had just slightly less than 100 employees in the year in which they do not appear on the tabulation, so that both of them had combined employments in excess of that of Firm C. If, for example, Firm B had had ninety workers in 1948 and Firm C had had ninety-five employees in 1947, their respective combined employments would have been 260 and 270—whereas that of Firm C is only 210. Firm C data are used because Firm C is the only large employer about which there is no uncertainty surrounding its operational existence in both mid-March periods. Therefore, the differentials may overstate the seriousness of the transitory element in the data but they cannot understate it.

Four of the twenty-five high concentration areas had different largest units in 1947 and 1948. Two of these were situations not unlike the above hypothetical case—that is, the employer identification codes indicated that the largest firms in these areas were different in the two years, but similarities in employment size and industry classification suggested that these were only nominal changes. These two areas had differentials above 90 per cent and thus accounted for the major portion of that sample's average differential. If the transitory differential of these two areas were changed to zero—i.e., if it were assumed that the largest units were the same in each period and that the change in ownership should not be considered as affecting those firms' stabilized market positions—the average differential of the twenty-five area sample for the single largest employer would

The transitory differentials provide information about transitory elements influencing concentration over the one-year interval beginning at the middle of March, 1947, and ending at approximately the same time in March, 1948. But this information is based completely on data gathered at the beginning and end of that time period. Hence it provides no clues as to the nature of those transitory elements that are of a seasonal character.

Accurate estimates of the effect of seasonality on concentration levels of individual areas cannot be made, for they would require much more detailed local area data than are available. However, an analysis of seasonal employment patterns between 1946 and 1950 by Woytinski[36] permits a rough calculation of the direction and magnitude of the necessary correction. The findings of significance for this purpose are these: there was a fairly constant pattern throughout the period which involved a "low" in the first quarter and a "high" in July and August; the average seasonal increment amounted to about 6.5 per cent of the average total employed labor force at the increment's maximum point;[37] and the industries accounting for the major portion of seasonal jobs were agriculture (by far the most important), construction, and retail trade. These industries are primarily small-firm industries so the major effect of increases in the number of workers employed by them would be corresponding increases in the denominators of concentration ratios with relatively rare effects upon numerators.

Therefore, if concentration ratios for the whole (five-year) period were available on a monthly basis, it is probable that they would follow a seasonal pattern that is roughly the opposite of the total employment pattern: namely, with a high in the first quarter and a low, probably about 5 per cent less than the peak, in mid-summer. The "stabilized" concentration

decline from 9.96 per cent to 2.32 per cent, and the rank correlation coefficient between the rankings of these areas according to 1947-48 average ratios and combined 1947-48 ratios would rise from the +.74 mentioned in the text to +.99. The differential for the four areas from that sample with enough large units to permit computation of the four-largest-units differential would not be affected.

36. W. S. Woytinski and associates, *Employment and Wages in the United States* (New York: The Twentieth Century Fund, 1953), pp. 336-41.

37. *Ibid.*, pp. 336-41 and 675-77. Average seasonal increments are presented in Table 115; the average total employed labor force was obtained by averaging the annual averages presented in Appendix Table 69.

positions would relate to neither the seasonal peak nor the trough; presumably, they would lie somewhere in between.

Applying Woytinski's methods and data to the thirteen month interval, March, 1947, through March, 1948, proves it to be typical. The maximum seasonal increment, less the average of the seasonal increments for March, 1947, and March, 1948, is 6.3 per cent of the average of the thirteen monthly total labor force figures.[38]

These rough calculations indicate that adjustment for seasonality in the concentration ratios of this paper would probably involve lowering all ratios 2 or 3 per cent if all areas were equally affected. Since, however, the agricultural component of the total seasonal variation completely dominates all others, since agriculture tends to be relatively more important in less populous labor market areas, and since concentration tends to be inversely related to size of labor force, it seems probable that the seasonal adjustment would reenforce the tendency of the non-seasonal transitory adjustment to decrease concentration more among the areas of high concentration.[39]

11. The Firm-Establishment Adjustment

The purpose of this section is two-fold, that of describing in greater detail the procedure for obtaining firm concentration ratios and presenting certain additional details of the thirty-two area sample investigation.

First: the procedure for preparing firm concentration ratios. Two data sources are needed. One of these is the Time-Series, the tabulation from which employment data for reporting units hiring 100 or more workers were obtained. Among other information provided for each reporting unit in the Time-Series is an individual employer identification number and a multiple-unit code (which indicates whether the unit is a single-establishment firm or a single unit in a multi-establishment firm). The other data source used in this connection is a supplementary tabulation called the "Zero Balance." (Located in the Employer Section, Statistics Branch of the

---

38. *Ibid.* The seasonal increments for March, 1947, and March, 1948, were 776,000 and 536,000 respectively; the maximum seasonal increment occurred in June, 1947, and amounted to 4,330,000. The average of the thirteen monthly total employed labor force figures was 58,233,000.

39. See Section 8 of this appendix for sample evidence supporting this suggestion that the decrease in concentration might be slightly greater in areas of higher concentration.

BOASI, this tabulation is labeled as follows: "Job 8055, Operation 037, Zero Balancing.") It is a listing of multi-unit firms, by employer identification codes, which provides the location and employment (as well as other data) of the constituent establishments.

The first step in converting the existing concentration ratios of an area into firm concentration ratios consists of checking the multiple-unit codes of those among the ten largest reporting units which had 100 or more employees; the Time-Series is used here, of course. No further action is taken in regard to those reporting units shown not to be members of a multi-unit firm. But if a multi-unit establishment is found, it is investigated further in the Zero Balance. There the geographic codes of the other establishments in the firm are examined to see if any of them are located in the same labor market area; if not, the concentration ratios already computed stand as firm concentration ratios. If there are other establishments of the same firm in the area, the units are combined, firms reranked, and concentration ratios for the area recomputed.

Employer data for firms hiring less than 100 workers were obtained from Table 615—a tabulation which does not provide individual reporting unit data. Therefore, it was not possible to check these units in the Zero Balance. This means that those areas in which there were less than ten establishments with 100 or more employees could not be given a "complete" firm-establishment check.

Second: in Chapter II, Section 3, of the text it was suggested that little change in the concentration ratios of this study would be brought about by putting them all on a firm rather than an establishment basis. The following additional details of the thirty-two area sample investigation tend to support that conclusion:

A. In figuring the original concentration ratios, data for 320 reporting units (the 10 largest in each of the 32 areas) were used. Of these, 118 (37 per cent) had employment of 100 or more workers: the firm-establishment check could be made for all of these areas—but for none of the 202 other "establishments" which hired less than 100 workers each.

Of the 118 reporting units, 61 were establishments in multiple-unit firms; of the 61 only 10 actually were located in the same area as another establishment of the same firm.

Thus less than one out of every 10 establishments investigated (10/118) was involved in a combination action.

B. Although the check could not be made on many of the "establishments" that ranked among the top ten in some of the areas, the check was complete for the single largest firm concentration ratios—since all areas included in the study contained at least one establishment hiring 100 or more workers. This complete adjustment brought about an average increase of only 3.4 per cent in concentration ratios. In the same vein, 79 of the 128 establishments used in computing the sample's four firm concentration ratios were units employing more than 100 workers—so the firm-establishment check could be made on all of these; since the average increase in concentration resulting from putting these on a firm basis was only 1.75 per cent, it is unlikely that adjusting the other 49 (smaller) units would increase this figure greatly. These considerations support the conclusion that the 5 per cent estimate in the text above is an overstatement.

C. Most of the areas (26 out of 32) were unaffected by the adjustment—the firm-establishment differential for all concentration ratios in these areas was zero.

12. FURTHER DETAILS OF THE COVERAGE EXPERIMENTS

The purpose of this section is that of adding several details concerning data or procedures to the discussion in Chapter II, Section 5.

1. It was pointed out that 40.5 per cent of the employed labor force in 1948 were not working for firms covered by OASI. This estimate was taken from the *Social Security Bulletin* article footnoted in the text; the underlying data were estimated for "an average week" in 1948.

For the 1,774 areas included in this study, the total employed labor force was about 52.0 million of which approximately 18.5 million (35.6 per cent) were not covered by Old-Age and Survivors Insurance. Thus the omission of about one-third of the smaller counties from this study decreased not-covered employment proportionately more than covered employment. The data from which this estimate was made are only roughly comparable with the *Social Security Bulletin* data; they relate to mid-March, 1948, and were used to obtain the estimate as follows: the 52.0 million is the sum of the estimated total employed labor forces of the 1,774 areas; from this

162 APPENDIX

was deducted the total of the workers covered by Old-Age and Survivors Insurance in the 1,774 areas; the difference between the totals was approximately 18.5 million.

2. The largest component of not-covered employment as shown in text Table 1 is in agriculture; the figure, 7.9 million. This was dismissed as a serious source of error in concentration ratios on the assertion that agriculture is a small-firm industry. Three bits of information gleaned from sample data in the 1950 Census support this generally-accepted characterization: the categories used for presentation of data concerning farms by number of workers hired were 1, 2, 3-4, 5-9, and 10 or more; the average number of hired workers per reporting farm was 2.2; and the percentage of farms in the 10 or more (employees) category was 2.2. See: U.S., Bureau of the Census, *United States Census of Agriculture: 1950* (Washington: U.S. Government Printing Office, 1952), II, 278.

3. In order to overestimate the total employment in each of the types of not-covered firms—railroad companies, hospitals, private educational institutions, public educational institutions, and governments—it was assumed that there was no more than one such firm in each labor market area; the employments of these firms were further assumed to be identical, respectively, with the 1948 employment in these industry groups: railroads and railway express service, medical and other health services, educational services, private, educational services, government, and public administration. The estimates of the 1948 employment in these "firms" were made for each area by multiplying the ratio of the 1948 total employed labor force (estimated) to the 1950 total employed labor force (provided in the census) by the number of employed workers in the 1950 Census in these industry groups. (U.S., Bureau of the Census, *1950 Census of Population. General Characteristics,* Series P-B preprints of Volume II, Table 43.)

4. The division of all government employees into two categories—public educational institutions and public administration—represents a conservative answer to a question which is almost as difficult as the matter of the appropriateness of introducing government as an employer in an investigation of monopsony. This concerns the definition of a government "firm," as illustrated by the following questions: In an area in which there are several agencies of each of the federal,

state, and local governments, what should be the operational definition of the "government firm?" Should each agency be considered separately? Should all agencies of any particular level of government (e.g., federal) in each area be combined into a single hiring unit? Should those agencies doing closely related types of work be combined regardless of the level of government they represent?

5. Finally, it should be noted that consideration was given to the use of all-BOASI concentration ratios (concentration ratios, that is, in which the denominators as well as the numerators are taken from BOASI sources) as the basic data of this study. Such ratios were actually computed and used in connection with certain experiments described in Chapter II. Their use would not, of course, have disposed of the problem of excluded firms. Nevertheless, such ratios have several appealing characteristics: such problems of exclusion as exist are identical for both numerators and denominators; the workers of both numerators and denominators are assigned, geographically, by the same criterion—place of employment; and the concentration ratios are simple to compute.

The case for using census rather than BOASI denominators has both negative and positive aspects: (1) It seems clear that BOASI concentration ratios would significantly overstate the absolute level of concentration because of the fact that BOASI numerators understate the "real-world" or "true" numerators by much less than BOASI denominators understate the "real-world" denominators; this is indicated by the small-firm bias of the exclusions. (2) Both BOASI and census denominators are surely different from the "true" denominators. For purposes of ranking areas these differences are important only to the extent that they vary—a set of denominators all of which are 25 per cent less than "true" denominators will, numerators being the same, provide identical rankings with "true" denominators. The issue, then, revolves around the question as to which set of denominators varies most consistently in magnitude and direction from the "true" denominators. It was decided that census denominators were probably more satisfactory in this regard. (3) The use of census denominators makes it possible to employ the Overall-Maximum bracketing process as a device which partially compensates for the absence of skill breakdowns in firm employment data.

13. The Use of Unadjusted Concentration Ratios for Ranking Labor Market Areas

In Chapter II, Section 6, it was pointed out that the agricultural not-skilled, the transitory, and the firm-establishment adjustments to sample data had brought about little change in the rankings of labor market areas by concentration. No mention was made in this discussion of rank changes caused by the excluded firms adjustments. In fact, no "before" and "after" rank correlation coefficients were computed for these adjustments. The reason for this has to do with the fact that the procedure used for these adjustments involved the "assumption" that all workers in certain census categories (e.g., "railroads and railway express service") were employees of a single firm. This is completely legitimate for obtaining adjustments designed to serve the purpose of not understating the change in the *level* of concentration. But since there "really" might often be two or more firms in some of the areas and since the added number of firms might either increase or decrease the numerical value of the coefficient relating adjusted and unadjusted rankings, "before" and "after" rank correlation comparisons would not have the same significance for the excluded firms adjustments as for the firm-establishment and other adjustments, each of which provides a rank correlation coefficient that is as low as it possibly can be within the confines of the sample data.

This may be illustrated by means of a simple hypothetical example. Consider five areas that have a given concentration rank order before the agricultural not-skilled adjustment. Performing this adjustment will bring about certain clear-cut changes in the denominators of Maximum ratios which, in turn, will have certain effects upon the rankings of areas by Maximum ratios. Given the desirability of making the adjustment, there is no ambiguity whatsoever in the results; it is certain that the new rankings correctly indicate the effect of the adjustment on the relative positions of the areas. No such certainty attaches to the railroad adjustment, however. Consider the same five areas and assume that the number of railroad workers in each is such that the adjustment causes the Overall-4 concentration ratios to rise by a flat 10 per cent—thereby leaving the rank order of the five areas unchanged. But this result came about because all railway workers in each area were accepted as employees of a single firm. If, in fact, there were several railway firms in, say, two of the areas, none of which were large enough to displace one of the four largest firms of the two areas, then these two Overall-4 ratios would not be changed and the "true" rank order of the five areas might be altered considerably as a result of the adjustment.

In spite of the factors discussed in the preceding paragraphs, it was stated in the text (Chapter II, Section 6) that the rankings of unadjusted concentration ratios were probably satisfactory for the analytical purposes of Chapter III. This conclusion is based on what is known about the private sector adjustments—as indicated by the rank correlation coefficients—in addition to what can be inferred from the railroad data. In regard to the latter, the low differentials found in the high concentration areas and the probability of overstatement among the differentials of the random sample areas make rank dislocation unlikely—as a widespread problem of serious magnitude, that is. Of course, all rankings will become considerably more suspect if future research should indicate that government and non-profit firms are not to be distinguished from private firms in regard to monopsonistic activity.

14. THE DIFFERENCE BETWEEN RANKINGS BY OVERALL AND MAXIMUM CONCENTRATION RATIOS

It was pointed out in Section 3 of Chapter III that the crucial factor in explaining the differences between rankings of areas by Overall and Maximum concentration ratios was the relative importance of agricultural workers in the employed labor force. This conclusion was drawn from an analysis of the rankings of the 105-area random sample by Overall-4 and Maximum-4 concentration ratios. The sample was broken into three groups of areas: those whose Maximum-4 concentration rankings were higher than their Overall-4 rankings by more than three ranks (group "A"); those whose Maximum-4 concentration rankings were neither above nor below their Overall rankings by more than three ranks (group "B"); and those whose Maximum-4 concentration rankings were lower than their Overall rankings by more than three ranks (group "C"). There were thirty-two areas in group

"A," thirty-one areas in group "B," and forty-two areas in group "C."

The "not-skilled," as that term was used for purposes of determining the denominators of Maximum concentration ratios, was computed as a percentage of the total employed labor force for all areas, and the averages of these percentages for the three groups of areas were found. The group "A" average was smallest and the group "C" average was largest. These results are not surprising: the denominator for the Overall ratios of an area is defined as its total employed labor force; the Maximum denominator is the not-skilled component of the employed labor force; if the not-skilled component is a fixed proportional amount of the total, say, one-half, areas will be ranked the same according to any of the three pairs of Overall-Maximum concentration measures (Overall-4 and Maximum-4, for example); if the not-skilled component varies as a proportion of the total, those areas having "average" not-skilled components will tend to be ranked by the Maximum measures in about the same way as they are ranked by Overall measures, those areas having "larger than average" not-skilled components will be ranked low by Maximum measures in comparison with their Overall rankings, and those areas having "smaller than average" not-skilled components will be ranked high by Maximum measures in comparison with their Overall rankings.

The accompanying chart shows the average not-skilled and skilled percentages for the three groups. The "skilled," as used in this connection, consists of the non-agricultural skilled workers (professional, managerial, and skilled) and *all* agricultural workers (owners, paid workers, and unpaid family workers). The question is, which of these skilled components "accounts" for the observed variation in the averages of unskilled percentages? Looking at the averages of the non-agricultural skilled first, it is clear that the deduction of this group of workers, by itself, from the total employed labor force would tend to produce variation in the unskilled percentages in the reverse of that shown in the chart. The deduction of the agricultural component by itself would, however, tend to produce variation in not-skilled percentages like that shown in the chart.

Group	Percentage of Not-Skilled	Percentage of Skilled	
		Non-Agricultural	Agricultural
A	36.1	19.5	43.9
B	50.0	27.7	20.9
C	55.7	29.4	14.1

Thus for purposes of deciding which means of ranking areas by concentration is preferable for some particular purpose, the issue may be more clearly drawn by describing the difference between the rankings in this fashion: Maximum concentration ratios provide rankings more closely approximating rankings based upon ratios derived from the non-agricultural component of the labor market than do Overall concentration ratios. This form of the conclusion about the relationship between Maximum and Overall rankings was checked on a small sample basis. Areas were arranged in the same fashion as for the selection of the 105-area sample (see Section 10 of this appendix); a twenty-area sample was obtained by selecting every eighty-fifth area. Concentration ratios having the largest firm as numerators and the employed non-agricultural labor force as denominators were computed. The twenty areas were ranked according to these ratios and according to Overall-1 ratios and Maximum-1 ratios. The following rank correlation coefficients were derived: Overall-1, Non-agricultural-1: $+.87$; Maximum-1, Non-agricultural-1: $+.97$.

15. THE 100-AREA COMPARATIVE SAMPLE

The 100-area sample used for comparative purposes in Section 6 of Chapter III was drawn in the following manner:

A. The 100 top concentration areas were ranked by labor force size from small to large.

B. The area that had the smallest labor force among the top 100—call it area "A"—was located on a tabulation of all 1,774 areas ranked by labor force size. The area *next above* area "A" was selected for the comparative sample; if this area happened to be one of the top 100 areas also, the area next above it was selected.

C. The next-to-smallest area among the top 100—call it area "B"—was located on the tabulation of 1,774 areas. The area *next below* it was selected for the comparative sample; if this area happened to be one of the top 100 areas also, the area next below it was selected.

TABLE 41

LABOR FORCE RELATIVE FREQUENCY DISTRIBUTIONS OF THE 100
COMPARATIVE AREAS BY COMMUNITY SIZE AND INDUSTRY

Industry	Percentage Distribution of Labor Force[a] for Areas in Three Community Size Classes[b]		
	0-5,499	5,500-12,499	12,500 and Over
Agriculture	37.1	34.5	10.8
Mining	1.4	3.3	3.0
Construction	6.9	5.4	7.8
Manufacturing	16.7	15.4	20.3
Transportation	4.8	5.3	7.9
Wholesale and retail trade	12.6	14.5	19.9
Finance, insurance, and real estate	1.0	1.4	2.9
Business and personal services	4.0	4.5	6.4
Professional and related services	5.8	7.1	8.5
All other[c]	9.7	8.6	12.5
Total	100.0	100.0	100.0
Aggregate labor force size[d]	102,042	293,413	965,400
Number of areas	34	33	33

[a] U.S., Bureau of the Census, *County and City Data Book, 1952: A Supplement to the Statistical Abstract of the United States* (Washington: Government Printing Office, 1953), Table 3.
[b] See note "a," Table 17.
[c] See note 'd," Table 18.
[d] These totals are sums of the 1948 labor force estimates (Overall denominators).

D. These steps were repeated until the 100 top areas had
been "duplicated." The resulting comparative sample contained none of the 100 top areas but the areas in it were much
like the areas of the 100 top areas as regards labor force size.

(This sampling procedure was suggested by Professor
Dudley J. Cowden.)

For reference purposes Table 41 presents relative frequency distributions of the labor force of the 100 comparative
areas by industry for each community size category used in
Table 18; in addition, the aggregate labor force size and
number of areas in each of the community size classes are
provided.

The 100 comparative areas were used in several ways.
One of these was to serve as a connecting link between the 100
high concentration areas and all areas of the United States,
as in Table 19. The comparability of the concentration characteristics of the comparative areas with "all areas" was
checked in the following fashion: all 1,774 areas were distributed among three labor force size categories the class

limits of which were chosen in such a way as to put 30 per cent of the areas in the small and large size categories and 40 per cent in the medium size category. The Maximum-4 medians for the three groups were twenty-five, twenty-one, and eighteen (small, medium, and large, respectively). The 100 comparative areas, distributed among the same three size categories, had medians that were roughly comparable: twenty-seven, twenty-two, and fourteen. The fact that this sample was drawn with the restriction that it could not contain any of the top 100 areas does not appear to have greatly influenced its level of concentration as indicated by this measure.

This check is not completely satisfactory. It consists of a comparison of the concentration characteristics of the 100 comparative areas and those of the whole group of areas studied; but the data in Table 19 refer literally to all areas in the United States and therefore are not identical in labor force coverage with the 1,774 areas of this study.

The comparative-area sample was also used in connection with the investigation of the reality of the community-size-concentration relationship. Both its small size bias and its industry structure played a part in that discussion. The argument made there is weakened by two characteristics of that sample. First, by the fact that its small size bias is not very strong; and second, by the fact that the industry structure of the areas is biased away from the high concentration industries, because the 100 high concentration areas were excluded from the universe from which the comparative areas were taken.

16. A Test of Monopsony Theory

The focus of attention of this study has been upon the development and analysis of concentration measures. However, in the basic BOASI sources there are certain "wage" data that made possible a test of the concentration-monopsony hypothesis. The comparability characteristics of these data are such that it was considered highly desirable to make this test, despite the fact that in certain other respects the data leave much to be desired.

In brief, the test consisted of two similar experiments. In the first, simple correlation coefficients were computed for concentration measures and wages in areas where the nine high concentration industries were earlier shown to be important. The second experiment consisted of a slightly more intensive examination of wages in one of these industries, using other wage-determining variables along with concentration.

The two most important measures needed for these experiments were local labor market indicators of concentration and of wages. The first of these was computed from the same summarizing formula used in Section 3, Chapter III, for choosing the "top 100" areas: $C' = 2x_1 + 4.5x_4 + 3x_{10}$. Specifically, for each labor market area used in these experiments the three Overall ratios (0-1, 0-4, and 0-10) were substituted for the x's (x_1, x_4, and x_{10}, respectively) of the summarizing formula. The resulting numbers measure, for each market, that portion of the area under the Overall concentration curve associated with the ten highest-ranking firms.[40]

Table 615 is one of the basic tabulations from which firm employment figures, as needed for the numerators of concentration ratios, were obtained. The same tabulation provides quarterly wage data of reporting firms, by state, county, and industry. By dividing the mid-March employment of the firms in state-county-industry classes into the total first quarter wages paid by those firms, "average" quarterly "wage" figures can be obtained for workers by industry and labor market area. In one county of South Carolina, for example, this tabulation showed four firms in industry group "22" ("Textile mill products") with combined mid-March, 1948, employment of 3,753; the total taxable payrolls, January through March, 1948, of these firms was $2,191,000. Thus the "average wage" for textile workers in that county was $2,191,000/3,753 or $586.00.[41]

40. It should be noted that this measure is a simpler one than that used in Chapter III. There the index was the arithmetic mean of the areas under the Overall and Maximum concentration curves.

41. The strengths and weaknesses of the wage data for the purpose at hand are rather clear-cut. On the "plus" side there is the comparability factor mentioned at the outset of this chapter: the wage data come from the same employer reports as the firm employment data used in the preparation of concentration ratios. Also, the data are broadly available, can be accurately allocated by county and industry, and are of high technical quality. On the "minus" side are some serious shortcomings. First, these average quarterly wage figures were obtained by dividing mid-March, 1948, employment into total taxable payrolls, January through March, 1948; the appropriate dividend, not available, is *average* first quarter, 1948, employment. Second, even if the average were properly computed, it would be a weak figure for present purposes—in comparison, for example, with straight-time average hourly earnings. Third, most of the data were available on a two-digit industry basis only. Finally, taxable payrolls cover payments only

The first experiment consisted of nine simple correlation computations, using the wage and concentration measures described above. The industry findings of the preceding chapter were used in the selection of labor market areas to be included in the computations. One state was selected for each of the nine most concentrated industries; in each case it was the state containing the most covered employees in the industry in 1948.[42] Within each of these states, counties were selected for investigation if they contained one or more firms (in the particular high concentration industry) that hired as many as 100 workers. For each of these nine groups of counties simple correlation coefficients between concentration and wages were computed. The results, with supplementary details, are presented in Table 42.

What sorts of results would Table 42 have to show in order to provide support for the concentration-monopsony hypothesis? It is probable that there would be disagreement among students of labor markets as to the expected magnitude of the

up to the first $3000 paid to any one employee. (Since almost all of the average wage figures were substantially less than $1000, this last point is not of serious consequence.)

42. This rule was not adhered to rigidly. Thus Pennsylvania had more covered employment in mining than West Virginia. West Virginia was used for two reasons: the isolation of some of the mining communities in that state makes it especially interesting for purposes of an investigation of monopsony; moreover, Pennsylvania also ranked highest in employment in Primary Metal Industries and thus separately qualified for inclusion in these computations. The other case of this sort was New Jersey, which was chosen despite the fact that it was slightly below New York in covered employment in "chemicals"; for New York was also the top-ranking state in "paper" and was selected to provide data for that industry.

Three modifications of the nine high concentration industries were made for purposes of these computations. In West Virginia "bituminous and other soft coal" was used rather than the whole industry group "mining"; in Pennsylvania "blast furnaces, steel works, etc." was used rather than the whole industry group "primary metal industries"; and in Michigan "motor vehicles and equipment" was substituted for the large industry group "transportation equipment."

The number of firms and their employments used in the wage computations of the selected labor market areas are as follows:

State	Number of firms	Total employment
North Carolina	966	238,550
Ohio	1,712	219,069
Michigan	335	432,365
Oregon	2,870	72,091
West Virginia	1,348	126,587
New York	941	64,561
Pennsylvania	100	202,169
Illinois	649	128,681
New Jersey	765	80,759

TABLE 42

COEFFICIENTS OF SIMPLE CORRELATION BETWEEN "WAGES"[a] AND CONCENTRATION[b] FOR LABOR MARKET AREAS[c] CONTAINING NINE HIGH CONCENTRATION INDUSTRIES

State	Industry	Number of Observations[d]	Coefficient of Simple Correlation	Coefficient of Determination
North Carolina	Textile mill products	62	+.029	.001
Ohio	Machinery (except electrical)	43	+.308	.095
Michigan	Transportation equipment[e]	32	+.035	.001
Oregon	Lumber and wood products	28	+.541	.293
West Virginia	Mining[f]	24	+.123	.015
New York	Paper and allied products	24	+.097	.009
Pennsylvania	Primary metal industries[g]	17	+.177	.031
Illinois	Electrical machinery	16	−.252	.063
New Jersey	Chemicals and allied products	6	−.804	.647

a "Wages" are computed for each labor market area by dividing mid-March, 1948, covered employment in the designated industry into the total January-March, 1948, taxable payrolls of firms in that industry.

b Computed for each labor market area using this formula: $C' = 2(0\text{-}1) + 4.5(0\text{-}4) + 3(0\text{-}10)$, where the symbols in parentheses refer to the three primary Overall concentration ratios.

c Areas used in these computations are those in which there is at least one firm in the designated industry of firm-size "100 and over."

d Each labor market area constitutes one observation.

e Only data from "Motor vehicles and equipment" were used in this industry group.

f Only data from "Bituminous and other soft coal" were used in this industry group.

g Only data from "Blast furnaces, steel works, etc." were used in this industry group.

coefficients—i.e., as to the proportion of the observed variation in wages which should be explainable in terms of this hypothesis. But there surely would be no disagreement concerning the signs of the coefficients. The more consistently they are negative, at respectable levels of significance, the greater the support provided for the hypothesis. In actual fact, seven of the nine coefficients have positive signs—higher concentration in these data tends to be associated with higher wages; and the two negative signs are attached to the numbers representing the smallest two samples in the experiment. In this same vein it should be noted that only two of the coefficients (those of Ohio and Oregon) are statistically significant at the 5 per cent level—and both of these are positive. The coefficients of simple correlation show a substantial amount of variation (from −.804 to +.541) but they seem to be centered around small positive numbers.

The relationship that seems to be showing itself through the data is a weak positive one. The discrepancy between this evidence and the results predicted by the concentration-monopsony hypothesis should be stated in these terms: the data fail to support the theory. This statement leaves open the possibility that there actually is a concentration effect tending to depress wages. For it may be that there are other variables that are so correlated with wages and concentration as to obscure this wage-concentration relationship. Or, of course, it may be that the shortcomings of the wage data are so serious as to make them relatively useless for an analysis such as this.

The next experiment consisted of an effort to probe deeper into the data in order to get at some of the questions left unanswered by the above investigation—especially the two problems raised in the preceding paragraph. For these purposes the largest of the state-industry samples above, the North Carolina-textiles sample of 62 observations, was used. It was expanded to 90 observations by applying the same labor market area selection criterion to South Carolina; there were 28 markets in that state containing at least one textile firm hiring 100 or more workers, so these were added to the sample. For all 90 areas the following measures were computed:

Y_1—average quarterly wages of textile workers for the first quarter 1948.

X_1—index of concentration figured from the summary formula, using Overall concentration ratios.

X_2—community size: estimated employed labor force, mid-March, 1948, in hundreds. (This is the denominator of Overall concentration ratios, expressed in hundreds.)

X_3—mean mid-March, 1948, employment of textile firms.

X_4—male textile workers as a percentage of all textile workers; computed from census data.[43]

Simple correlation coefficients among these variables were computed as follows:

$$r_{YX_1} = +.126$$
$$r_{YX_2} = +.219$$
$$r_{YX_3} = +.238$$
$$r_{YX_4} = +.392$$

43. U.S. Bureau of the Census, *1950 Census of Population. General Characteristics.* Series P-B preprints of Volume II, Table 43.

The standard error of r's figured from samples of size 90 drawn from a population in which the variables are unrelated is .106. Thus r_{YX_1} is the only one of the above four r's which is not statistically significant at the 5 per cent level. This provides a basis for some confidence in the wage data. For the influence of the three additional variables upon wages has been documented well enough to permit predictions of such positive coefficients as these.

This result underlines the importance of the other matter of concern about the data, however: are there variables which are so related to concentration and wages separately as to obscure the relationship between the two? To throw light upon this matter the above variables were put into a multiple regression framework. The linear least squares equation is

$$Y = 253 + .060X_1 + .105X_2 + .014X_3 + 4.400X_4$$

standard errors of				
regression coefficients	.103	.047	.023	1.228
multiple correlation coefficients	.126	.262	.315	.466
coefficients of determination	.016	.069	.099	.217

Comparison of the net regression coefficients with their standard errors suggest reappraisal of only one of the simple correlation results: the coefficient for "firm size" is smaller than its standard error, indicating that the r_{YX_3} of +.238 was partially a reflection of a relationship among firm size, wages, and one of the other independent variables. The regression coefficients of community size and the percentage of male workers are more than two and three times their respective standard errors, however, indicating their significance for wage determination in the presence of the other independent variables. The sign and size (relative to its standard error) of the concentration regression coefficient provide support for the previous simple correlation findings and suggest that these particular other wage determining variables, at least, are not hiding a concentration effect.

The conclusion toward which all of the above explorations seem to be leading is that concentration is an unimportant factor in wage determination. The total level of "explained variation," as shown by the above coefficients of determination, remains fairly low, however. Confidence in the conclusion concerning the concentration effect upon wages would be increased if a larger proportion of the observed variation in wages could be accounted for without the net relationship between wages and concentration becoming significantly different from zero.

There is one possible source of what might be thought of as fortuitous variation in the dependent variable. That variable was prepared by dividing mid-March employment of textile firms into first quarter taxable payrolls of those firms. There undoubtedly are many situations in which variations in employment over the first quarter of 1948 were such as to make the mid-March employment figure an inaccurate substitute for average quarterly employment. It is probable that there was a good deal of cancellation of this effect in those markets containing large numbers of textile firms, but it could be a serious source of variation in the "averages" of textile wages obtained from markets containing small numbers of firms.

In order to see if this were the source of some of the "unexplained" variation in the results of the preceding multiple regression effort the experiment was repeated with this single change in the procedure: only those labor market areas were selected which contained at least three textile firms in the 100-499 employment size class. This reduced the number of "observations" from 90 to 37. The results were the following:

$$Y_1 = 329 + .101X_1 + .104X_2 + .144X_3 + 2.189X_4$$

standard errors of regression coefficients	.126	.041	.068	1.492
multiple correlation coefficients	.096	.549	.715	.736
coefficients of determination	.009	.301	.511	.542

The regression coefficient of the concentration variable is again less than its standard error, and once more the regression coefficients of two of the independent variables are more than twice their standard errors.[44] This continuity in result is made more significant by the fact that, as conjectured, the coefficient of determination moves upward appreciably.

44. In this case it is "community size" and "firm size" that show significant regression coefficients; in the preceding equation it was "community size" and "percentage of males." This aspect of the experiment was designed to remove fortuitous variation in the firm-size variable. It is to be expected that more accurate firm size indicators would show the firm size-wage relationship more clearly. Also it should be noted that the simple correlation coefficient for "firm size" and "percentage of males" is +.548 for the 37 areas of this experiment and +.294 for the 90 areas of the larger sample.

The preceding part of the experiment was interpreted to mean that there is, in fact, a good deal of variation in the wage figures resulting from the use of mid-March employment as a proxy for average first quarter employment. This, in turn, suggests that better results might be obtained by using data from a segment of the labor market in which average firm size is not so great—so that there will be greater opportunity for cancellation of employment variation among firms. The experiment was discontinued at approximately this point, however, so that the extent of improvement which could be brought about in this fashion cannot be accurately reported.

It is completely appropriate to use the word "exploratory" and the phrase "tentative findings" in connection with the efforts described in this section. But it is also important to stress the consistency with which they fail to provide support for the hypothesis. In this sense they constitute an additional empirical basis, drawn from a different level of analysis, for doubting that monopsonistic behavior is broadly characteristic of United States labor markets.

BASIC CONCENTRATION DATA FOR 1,774 LOCAL LABOR MARKET AREAS

(containing much of the basic data analyzed in Chapter III) This 84-page table, in Xerox form, may be procured at no cost by writing to either the author, Robert L. Bunting, Department of Economics and Business Administration, Cornell College, Mount Vernon, Iowa, or the publisher, The University of North Carolina Press, Chapel Hill, North Carolina.

INDEX

areas of intermediate size, 63-72; hypothetical bivariate distribution, 64; a possible explanation of, 70-72; independent of industry, 108

Commuting, and county combinations, 149-52; mentioned, 20-21

Complete-check counties, defined, 121, 122

Concentration, defined, 4; refining measures of, 8; and labor force size, 12, 98, 102; and firm size, 12, 98, 102; and industry, 12-13, 72-84, 98, 102, 106-8; and region, 13-14, 85-98, 102; distribution of areas toward low classes of, 43; within community size-region classes, 87-88; as dependent variable, 97; overstatement by Maximum ratios, 100; understated by Overall ratios, 100; findings summarized, 112-13

Concentration curves, defined, 8, 100; illustrated, 9; decision to investigate three points on, 9-10; bracketing of by Overall and Maximum ratios, 16. *See also* Bracketing

Concentration findings, used in test of hypothesis, 171. *See also* Concentration

Concentration, level of, as measured by areas, 44; as measured by employment, 46; comparison of area measures with employment measures, 46; appraised as not high, 47; mentioned, 12, 42, 43-47, 98, 102, 103

Concentration-monopsony hypothesis, stated, 4-6; test of, 113, 114, 169-76; mentioned, 47

Concentration ratios, and product monopoly, 6; illustrated, 10; expressed as percentages, 10; numerators, 11; denominators, 11; errors in, 14; labor markets computed for, 21; employment ratios vs. payroll ratios, 29-31; error in, 38-41; various adjustments to, 39-41; lack of independence, 47-48; agreement among in selection of high concentration areas, 50-53; areas common to top portions of six distributions, 52; as basic data, 99; shortcomings of data, 109-12; all-BOASI, 163; used in test of hypothesis, 170

Construction, seasonal effects, 25; industry, 127

Cook County, Illinois, 122

Correlations, concentration-community size and industry, 83

Counties, sizes of, 20, 135-36; as labor markets, 20-21, 99; excluded from study, 21; non-metropolitan combinations of, 21, 138

County Business Patterns, 1948, 4, 11, 16n, 29, 115, 116, 118, 125, 128, 154

Delinquent firms, as source of error in concentration ratios, 128

Delinquent reports tabulation, 116, 120

Demand, low cross-elasticity of, 19

Denominators, of Maximum ratios, 115, 117-18; of Overall ratios, 117, 128-29

Domestic service, exclusion, 32

East North Central region, 91, 94-97 *passim*

East South Central region, 86, 94-97 *passim*

Electrical machinery industry, 13, 82, 89, 90, 107, 108

Employed labor force, per cent studied, 99

Employer reports, first quarter (1948), 100-1

Employment, large-firm distribution of, among industries, 77-79; by industry of largest firms, and concentration, 77-80, 83-84; regional distribution of, by industry and community size, 91-93

Employment concentration ratios, as measures of dominance, top areas, 56; as measures of dominance, all areas, 61-62; vs. payroll ratios, 111; mentioned, 115

Entrepreneurial workers, deleted from Overall denominators, 100

Experiments, measurement of changes in rank positions of firms, 24; measurement of transitory factors in firm employment, 24; testing for regional concentration factor, 94-97

Farm laborers, excluded from Maximum denominators, 19

Firm employment, lack of occupational composition, 36

Firm-establishment adjustment, 37, 111, 112, 159-61

Firm size, non-mometary disadvantages of, 30

Firms, largest in high concentration areas, 21n; transitory elements in employment figures, 22-26; multi-unit, 26, 27; dominance among, as related to concentration, 42, 52, 55, 57-59,

www.ingramcontent.com/pod-product-compliance
Lightning Source LLC
Chambersburg PA
CBHW021558210326
41599CB00010B/500